in_focus

Comanagement
of Natural
Resources

in_focus

IDRC's *In_Focus* Collection tackles current and pressing issues in sustainable international development. Each publication distills IDRC's research experience with an eye to drawing out important lessons, observations, and recommendations for decision-makers and policy analysts. Each also serves as a focal point for an IDRC Web site that probes more deeply into the issue, and is constructed to serve the differing information needs of IDRC's various readers. A full list of *In_Focus* Web sites may be found at **www.idrc.ca/in_focus**. Each *In_Focus* book may be browsed and ordered online at **www.idrc.ca/books**.

IDRC welcomes any feedback on this publication. Please direct your comments to The Publisher at **pub@idrc.ca**.

Comanagement
of Natural
Resources

LOCAL LEARNING
FOR POVERTY REDUCTION

by Stephen R. Tyler

INTERNATIONAL DEVELOPMENT RESEARCH CENTRE

Ottawa • Cairo • Dakar • Montevideo • Nairobi • New Delhi • Singapore

Published by the International Development Research Centre
PO Box 8500, Ottawa, ON, Canada K1G 3H9
www.idrc.ca / info@idrc.ca

Library and Archives Canada Cataloguing in Publication

Tyler, Stephen R
Comanagement of natural resources : local learning for poverty reduction /
by Stephen R. Tyler.

Issued also in French under title: La cogestion des ressources naturelles.
Includes bibliographical references.

ISBN 1-55250-328-3

1. Natural resources—Comanagement—Developing countries—Case studies.
2. Conservation of natural resources—Developing countries—Case studies.
3. Conflict management—Developing countries—Case studies.
4. Sustainable development—Developing countries—Case studies.
5. Rural development—Developing countries—Case studies.
I. International Development Research Centre (Canada)
II. Title.

HD75.6.T94 2006   333.7   C2006-980260-2

IDRC Books endeavours to produce environmentally friendly publications.
All paper used is recycled as well as recyclable. All inks and coatings are
vegetable-based products.

This publication may be read online at **www.idrc.ca/books**, and serves as
the focal point for an IDRC thematic Web site on the comanagement of
natural resources: **www.idrc.ca/in_focus_comanagement**.

Contents

Foreword

In the past two decades we have seen dramatic developments in the understanding of equitable and sustainable natural resource management. These have been informed and backed by innovation and research, not least that supported by IDRC, Canada's International Development Research Centre. The old ideas of command and control, of blaming poor people for mismanagement of their resources, have been overturned. As this book shows, the results can be truly remarkable.

Researchers and other outsiders change their mindsets, behaviours, attitudes, and ideas about their roles. They become convenors, facilitators, negotiators, and supporters. Local people become the main actors, learners, managers, and owners of the process of change. The goals of equity for people who live at the margins, and of sustainable management, are approached and achieved by starting not with natural resources but with people, enabling them to empower themselves, and by coevolving systems of comanagement.

The evidence that such approaches work stands out from the cases reported in this book. The practical lessons are empirically based. These are not the fond imaginings of idealists but the hard findings of experience. And the outcomes, lessons, and practical implications are clearly and succinctly summarized.

The findings raise a challenge that must not be underestimated. They upend the beliefs and reverse the reflexes of many surviving and powerful professionals. The danger is that these insights will be rejected by a rearguard of some who are well-intentioned but out of touch and out of date. For they contradict the seductive lure of earlier approaches, which were simpler, more standard, and top-down. American journalist and satirist H.L. Mencken wrote, "To every problem, there is a solution which is simple, direct, and wrong." Control-oriented custodial management was simple and direct, and proved a local lose–lose solution. In contrast, the comanagement analyzed here is complex, evolutionary, and win–win for local people, with losers the would-be extractive exploiters from outside. Comanagement combines policy reforms, new institutions for local resource tenure and management, secure and equitable access to resources, and technological innovation to increase productivity. Comanagement works because it puts people at the centre, is emergent, is locally adapted and owned. It has no one blueprint but differs in each case and context, manifesting a creative diversity fitting local conditions.

This slim volume should be on the bookshelf of every policy-maker, practitioner, teacher, and trainer concerned with human development and natural resource management. But the bookshelf is not enough. The book should be read, internalized, and acted on. We, development professionals, are fortunate to have such a well-grounded, authoritative, and accessible contribution to learning and change. It brings us up to date and puts us on the frontier of action and learning. May it lead to many good things being done, enhancing equity and sustainability, and with gains to many of those who are poor and marginal seeking their livelihoods in fragile and vulnerable parts of our world.

Robert Chambers
June 2006

Robert Chambers is an expert in international development and a pioneer in participatory methodologies, especially for empowering the poor. Since 1972, he has been affiliated with the Institute of Development Studies, University of Sussex, Brighton, UK, where he is currently a research associate in the Participation Group. Author of the seminal 1983 work *Rural Development: Putting the Last First*, Chambers' most recent book, *Ideas for Development*, was published in 2005 by Earthscan.

.

Preface

Water, soil, air, nutrients, sunlight — these are the stuff of life.
And the amazing diversity of living species, linked in ways that
we sometimes only dimly understand, is what people everywhere
depend on for their existence. But a quick glance at almost any
newspaper suggests that, wherever you live, natural resources and
the people who depend on them are in trouble. Drought, floods,
erosion, deforestation, declining soil fertility, habitat loss, over-
exploitation — environmental change is proceeding at an alarm-
ing pace, driven by a range of factors including global climate.
But practical actions to respond to these issues are not as prominent. This book draws attention to local innovations to better
manage ecosystems that rural women and men rely on in some
of the poorest parts of the world.

The results and lessons reported here are from applied research
supported by Canada's International Development Research
Centre (IDRC) in different regions of the developing world. The
purpose of IDRC funding is to enable local researchers to find

solutions to their social, economic, and environmental problems. Since its creation in 1970, IDRC has supported research on many topics and in many sectors, including agriculture and natural resources. But it became clear in the mid-1990s that, despite research-driven gains in technical capacity and productivity, benefits were not reaching the rural poor as expected. The ecosystems on which they depended for food and commercial products continued to degrade. Resources they had used for centuries were claimed by outsiders. Traditional mechanisms for allocating access to resources were breaking down under demographic and market pressures. New production technologies were captured by the wealthiest social groups, squeezing out the poor. IDRC and its partners concluded that research intended to reduce environmental degradation and improve the livelihoods of the poor had to adopt a different approach to be effective. Some of the results from this different approach are presented here.

The stories in this volume represent a much larger corpus of research begun in the late 1990s. They have been selected to illustrate a wide range of political, economic, and ecological contexts. The resource base is different in each case, the problems vary, and the solutions are specific to the context. Some cases deal mainly with forest management, others with agriculture, water, fisheries, or pastures. But the reader will find them easy to compare because they all adopt a common research framework based on participatory action and "learning-by-doing."

It turns out that the elaboration and testing of this common framework provided many of the most important lessons from the field. These are lessons not only for research but, more importantly, for practice. Too often, development professionals, whether local or expatriate, believe that only highly specialized experts can provide insights into complex local resource management problems. These cases demonstrate practical alternatives whereby external technical expertise serves to validate local knowledge, inform local action, and facilitate locally led initiatives. They also show that adaptive resource management requires everybody involved to learn, not just the researchers.

All of the cases demonstrate how local ingenuity and innovation can combine resource conservation with improved livelihoods. But in supporting local initiative, researchers have not turned their backs on government. Indeed, the crucial role of governments in creating enabling conditions, providing technical support, enforcing local management regimes, or at least preventing further conflict and degradation is evident in all the examples. That is why the title emphasizes "comanagement," or sharing management responsibilities between local users and governments. The hard part is figuring out how to build local capacity, engage researchers with resource users in testing new approaches, strengthen the livelihoods of the poorest, and ensure government officials understand the situation well enough to draw valid conclusions for policy reforms — all at the same time! These cases provide concrete examples.

This book is also about poor farmers and fishers, the men and women so often considered the bottom rungs of the social ladder. It is a book about their creativity, commitment, and initiative as much as that of the researchers. Their stories are reason for optimism: given opportunity, knowledge, and secure access to resources, people will choose to invest in common efforts to conserve those assets and sustain their livelihoods.

Writing this book has only been possible because of the efforts of dozens of field-based researchers on the six project teams. Their work has been arduous, their understanding subtle — and I cannot possibly do justice to it in this slim volume. Wendy Manchur and Richard Bruneau did a great job in helping to select cases and in pulling together documentation. Gerry Toomey and Bob Stanley provided expert editorial services, and Bill Carman of IDRC's Communications Division gave professional guidance and coordinated the entire production. I am much indebted to them all in sharpening and strengthening this work, but accept responsibility for any errors or omissions.

Stephen R. Tyler
June 2006

Stephen R. Tyler is president of Adaptive Resource Management Ltd, a consulting and research firm based in Victoria, Canada. He is the editor of *Communities, Livelihoods and Natural Resources: Action Research and Policy Change in Asia*, copublished in 2006 by ITDG Publishing and IDRC. Dr Tyler was formerly team leader for IDRC's Community-based Natural Resource Management program in Asia. In that position, he was responsible for a portfolio of more than 75 projects in 12 countries over 7 years. He holds a doctorate in city and regional planning from the University of California in Berkeley and has worked on environment and resource management issues in Canada and other countries for almost 30 years.

Part 1

The Issue and Research Context

Fragile resources, forgotten people

Rugged mountains, desert margins, remote coastal villages —
these are typical hot spots of rural poverty in the developing
world. They are also places where natural resources,[1] though vital
to human livelihoods, are usually meagre and fragile.

People may have to scratch out a living on land that is steep,
rocky, dry, or saline. Or they may live near bodies of water in
which fish are harder and harder to catch. These farmers and
fishers are far from bustling markets, far from capital cities, far
from the minds and lives of the powerful. The ecosystems on
which they depend are being depleted of nutrients and stripped
of their biological diversity. And control of the valuable resources
that do remain is contested, sometimes violently.

Many developing countries have formally adopted national
poverty-reduction strategies. International donor agencies, too, in
step with the United Nations' Millennium Development Goals
for reducing poverty and improving living conditions by 2015,

---

[1] The term "natural resources" is used in this book to refer to renewable resources
as components of living ecosystems. The term may also include nonrenewable
mineral resources, which are not addressed here.

have set targets. Yet poverty-reduction strategies typically focus on broad reforms or on the delivery of services that do not reach the poorest, most marginal communities, which depend so heavily on natural resources.

The reform of agricultural markets and land titling are often recommended, for example, as part of a poverty-reduction package. Worthy policy efforts? Yes. But incentives such as low-cost credit to buy seed and fertilizer for cash-crop production are not designed to benefit those who live far from input and product markets, have no collateral, or lack skills to grow high-value crops. Even worse, land titling reforms may lead to enclosure and privatization of the remaining resources on which these people depend — so-called common pool resources such as water, fisheries, and forests. Although high-yielding crop varieties have greatly increased grain production and enriched lowland farmers with access to irrigation, they often fail in marginal areas where soils, water, and climate conditions are more variable. Or they place further demands for water and nutrients on already degraded ecosystems.

The poorest people on the planet live in these marginal rural areas. Global estimates of the number of rural poor subsisting in such environments range from 600 to 900 million, roughly 9% to 14% of world population. Without livelihood options, these people are forced to migrate to cities, to become refugees, or worse. If poverty-reduction targets are to be meaningful, these people's situation merits special attention.

Global estimates of the number of rural poor subsisting in marginal areas range from 600 to 900 million, roughly 9% to 14% of world population. Without livelihood options, these people are forced to migrate to cities, to become refugees, or worse.

How can the livelihoods of poor people be improved without further damaging the underlying resource base? How can the global goals of rural poverty reduction and environmental sustainability be made to complement each other rather than compete?

This book describes research, funded by Canada's International Development Research Centre (IDRC), which has led to innovative natural resource management (NRM) approaches that balance these two goals. With the aid of six case studies from Asia, the Middle East, and Latin America, it draws lessons for development practitioners, policymakers, and researchers.

The work relied heavily on the knowledge and experience of local people. It made them, rather than the researchers, the key agents of learning and change. A common thread in these projects was the resolution of natural resource management issues through "comanagement." This refers to arrangements whereby local people and their organizations are given responsibility for decision-making about access to and use of natural resources, in exchange for assured benefits, through agreements with government authorities.

Comanagement covers a spectrum of arrangements — from formal legal agreements that are politically negotiated to informal pragmatic deals. Sustainable local use of natural resources is comanagement's raison d'être. But as IDRC-supported research demonstrates, the key challenges have less to do with technical interventions than with managing relations among people (Figure 1). This has implications for scientists in their relationship with, and attitudes toward, poor resource users, as well as for development practitioners and government officials.

> Sustainable local use of natural resources is comanagement's raison d'être. But the key challenges have less to do with technical interventions than with managing relations among people.

The message delivered by the case experiences is simple: the most effective way to introduce comanagement of natural resources is to engage resource users and other local stakeholders in shared

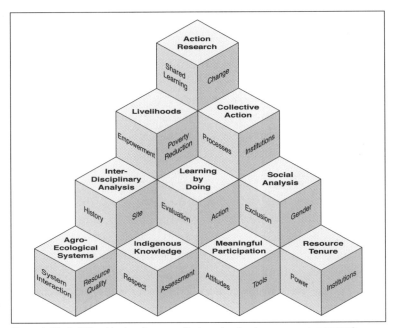

Figure 1. The building blocks of community-based natural resource management.

learning and innovation, which strengthens their livelihoods. Local knowledge, experience, and traditions of NRM are valuable assets when harnessed for research and action. Understanding and drawing on these assets leads to more successful NRM innovations than when local users are treated as uninformed bystanders to be handed technical solutions by "experts" and prepackaged regulatory schemes by governments. This process of participatory action research can be a powerful tool for comanagement innovation.

A little history, much complexity

The problems of how to pursue economic progress for the poor while protecting the environment were brought to world attention in 1987 in the report of the Brundtland Commission,

Our Common Future (WCED 1987). Then, in 1992, the issues were debated by global leaders at the UN Conference on Environment and Development in Rio de Janeiro, dubbed the Earth Summit. The conference report, Agenda 21, presented hundreds of recommendations for study and action to address the challenges, and attracted widespread international attention and financial commitment. Yet implementation of these proposals at the local level has proven elusive. Why?

Although poverty and environmental degradation are linked, their causal connections are anything but simple. Our understanding of nature is far from perfect and surprise is one of the few constants in human efforts to manage natural environments, which are complex and dynamic.

To this we must add the difficulty of predicting human behaviour in using resources. Interactions between socioeconomic systems and the natural environment are full of twists and turns — reflecting changing incentives afforded by markets and other institutions, and the dynamics of ecosystems themselves. For example, efforts to promote prawn aquaculture throughout Asia increased export earnings but also led to massive environmental damage in coastal areas. Many of the original production sites had to be abandoned because of disease or soil contamination. Market benefits have flowed mostly to external investors, while shrimp disease and degradation have rendered the resource base unusable to local people (Flaherty et al. 1999).

When the interaction of these complex systems degrades key resources, the effects may be felt even far away. Cutting forests or clearing new lands for farming in the headwaters of a watershed can affect water flow and quality downstream. Loss of habitat essential to the life cycle of commercial fish species can trigger the collapse of regional stocks. Draining wetlands can harm the quality of surface water or groundwater for thousands of users and destroy wildlife habitats. Overgrazing can speed desertification, endangering transportation corridors and other infrastructure. If resource degradation is widespread, it can contribute to regional or even global change. The other side of the coin is that protecting and rebuilding healthy ecosystems through local management benefits not only nearby resource users but also people in other regions and countries. In short, local management delivers public goods.

> Protecting and rebuilding healthy ecosystems through local management benefits not only nearby resource users but also people in other regions and countries. In short, local management delivers public goods.

The poor are particularly vulnerable to resource degradation and over-exploitation. Whether displaced by competition for vital resources or victimized by falling water tables as a result of the action of other water users, they generally have very few options and backup resources to cope with unexpected stress. A number of studies in South Asia demonstrate how agricultural intensification eliminated options previously available to the poor — harvesting weedy plants on field margins, gleaning unwanted fruits or nuts, use of communal pasture. These opportunities disappeared with the expansion of cultivated private land and more intensive commercial agriculture (Beck and Nesmith 2001).

Even as their access to these resources disappears, the poor have few opportunities to voice their outrage or describe impacts. Women often have limited influence on decision-making in local government or the household; yet they are on the frontlines in coping with resource degradation, changing production systems, and market access (Vernooy 2006). As members of ethnic minorities, Indigenous groups, and lower castes, the poor often face official and informal discrimination. This hampers their access to government services and decisions, especially if these are offered only in the language of the dominant culture. The rural poor are not only marginalized geographically, but politically and socially. How can they come to play a larger role in resource management?

Different resources, different rights

Comanagement options for poor marginal areas depend on several factors and how they interact: the nature of the resource to be managed, local rights to the resource, the institutions governing those rights and decision-making, and how the resources are exploited.

Some resources, such as cultivated land, are clearly defined and easily demarcated. The rights of access, use, and management are usually privately held by a single household. The household may own the land, hold it under long-term lease or customary agreement, or rent it. These private rights are clear, and they are closely tied to land-management practices. For example, farmers are unlikely to invest in costly improvements such as terracing unless they have secure land tenure, thus ensuring they will benefit over the long run. Institutions (traditional or government sanctioned) provide the framework of law or custom through which these private rights are recognized. And they establish rules governing the use or exchange of the resource. Land titling is an example.

Whereas the system of rights, institutions, and management practices may be clear for agricultural land, for other resources it is often much fuzzier. Many valuable resources are very difficult or costly for any individual to manage because of their ecological characteristics. The resource may be highly mobile (fisheries for example), it may only be practical to manage at a large scale (a watershed), or it may have many different elements that are used by different people (a forest). In many cases, it may be impractical to prevent any given individual from using the resource, even though that use subtracts from the benefits others can obtain (shared pasture). Resources with these characteristics are referred to as common pool resources or CPRs (Ostrom 1990; Pinkerton and Weinstein 1995).

Resource tenure (sometimes referred to as "property rights") is a claim that one person or group makes on a resource, and that other people or groups recognize as legitimate and enforceable. Tenure can take a wide variety of forms and cover a broad range of rights, depending on the nature of the resource, the social relationships between those involved, and the costs of enforcing claims of varying complexity. Tenure can be thought of as a bundle of rights, which may include any one or more of access, on-site use, harvest, and extraction of a resource, as well as the right to exclude other users, to set rules for resource use, to improve the resource (cultivation, fertilization), and to transfer any or all of these rights to others. The most comprehensive tenure is outright ownership, which encompasses all of these. But there are many other forms of tenure, which may overlap or conflict on any given territory or over time. For example, a single tree in the forest may provide fruit, firewood, fodder, shade, soil stability, wildlife habitat, and a link to ancestral identity. The rights to these different resources may be held by different individuals or groups at different times (Vandergeest 1997).

The problems of resource management and access by the poor often centre on CPRs and on the associated system of resource rights or tenure. Under certain conditions, systems of collective rights will be defined by groups who can control access to CPRs to increase their benefits and reduce degradation of the resource (Schlager and Ostrom 1992). Tropical forests, for example, may be intensively exploited by different users at different times. The harvested products range from wildlife and fruits to medicinal plants and construction materials, even if no timber is cut. Rangelands require collective management to allow different users to graze livestock under a rotation schedule to which all agree. The resources are used by individuals, but their ecological characteristics mean that to assure productivity they must be managed collectively. A framework established by a defined group of individuals to manage CPRs sustainably is often referred to as common property resource management.

There are many examples of CPRs being either weakly managed or not managed at all, where continuing exploitation by many users gradually erodes stocks. This kind of tenure is termed "open access." For the individual user, there is no incentive to conserve or manage the resource because other users simply capture the benefits of such conservation without paying the costs. The North American plains bison, for example, was hunted to virtual extinction in the 19th century. Many local and regional fisheries around the world are in a perilous state for the same reason.

The picture is further complicated because the same resources may be claimed by different groups under both common and private tenures at the same time. And as resource rights and management systems change, a resource may shift from one category to another. The forests of Nepal provide a good example. In the late 1950s, the government nationalized forests that had traditionally been locally managed under feudal landlords. Customary local rights to use the forest, which were bound up in feudal obligations, disappeared. But the government did not have enough staff or knowledge to enforce its new management rights, and communities were no longer under any long-term obligations to landlords. In effect, the status of the forests shifted to open access, resulting in a dramatic increase in deforestation. In the 1980s, after community forest tenures were formally introduced, local forest user groups gained the right to exclude others and to benefit from long-term forest management. The condition of forests improved dramatically in communities able to establish effective common property management institutions (Varughese 2000).

In areas of long-standing human occupation, cultures that depend on valuable CPRs well understand that the security of their resource base requires regulation. From the Arctic to the tropics, many cultures have developed complex local systems for allocating access to resources, sharing benefits, and limiting resource extraction. These systems were not based on modern scientific study; but they certainly reflected extensive local knowledge and experience (Berkes 1989; Ostrom 1990). In the Arsaal Valley of Lebanon, for example, traditional social relations governed herders' access to seasonal pastures of varying quality. Collective decisions allowed for flexible management according to pasture conditions (see page 60).

So the potential for resource management innovation rests partly on the rights of users, and partly on the characteristics of the ecosystem in question. Resource management is implemented through social institutions. We use the word "institutions" here to mean the conventional social processes and rules governing decision-making, not organizations or "bricks and mortar" structures. The institutions of resource management reflect prevailing social and political practices — how do people interact, who holds power, and how can it be legitimately used. They may be based on legal and judicial procedures, on religious beliefs, or on traditional practices. Institutions are the mechanisms by which societies define who can use the resource and who is excluded, and how access and benefits may be shared among rights holders. They also can provide mechanisms to resolve conflicts, track resource quality and identify problems, take measures to improve resource productivity, and enforce rules. These decisions are at the heart of resource management. In the case of CPRs, so important to the poor, who gets to make these management decisions?

Today, the management of CPRs is most often undertaken by governments. In many countries, legal frameworks that originated centuries ago in the claims of European monarchs dictate that any resources with no private title of ownership belong to the state. The expansion of scientific knowledge has been accompanied by greater emphasis on the need for specialized technical training to make resource-management decisions. It is also commonly argued that oversight and exercise of such expertise ought to reside in large, technocratic organizations rather than with uneducated local resource users. Resource management is seen as a service to be provided by the state — because it delivers public goods and because elements of a country's resource endowment are part of the national heritage, not the private property of individuals.

Nevertheless, in the past two decades, structural adjustment policies and fiscal restraint have led to deep cuts in government services. Centralized NRM has been weakened by budget reductions and by greater emphasis on private investment and resource exploitation. At the same time, however, traditional local systems of CPR management have been eroded by cultural change and by the legal institutions of the modern nation-state.

Even where central resource-management agencies have been strengthened, the local results are often disappointing. Central managers often lack essential data and may fail to understand local practices or the links between resource degradation, rights, and power relations. Management actions based on widely held assumptions about the resource base frequently turn out to be inappropriate. Changing conditions render well-intended regulations irrelevant. For example, in the El Angel watershed of Ecuador, official allocations of water resources were based on mistaken assumptions about water flows and availability (see page 44).

> Central managers often lack essential data and may fail to understand local practices or the links between resource degradation, rights, and power relations.

In many cases, the modern state-led management system has been laid over top of earlier colonial land administration. That in turn may have paid little attention to traditional resource-management practices, some of which persist in remote areas. Administrative boundaries rarely match either traditional territories or ecological boundaries such as watersheds.

Local resource users may not understand or agree with the legal policies and economic principles by which the state allocates resources for large-scale commercial extraction. Valuable resource rights may be allocated inequitably to politically powerful interests. As a result, rights to use and manage the resource are contested, with the state, as the legal manager, sometimes finding itself in opposition to local people's interests. The poor, who are often ethnic minorities and Indigenous peoples, are typically on the losing end of these contests. In the upland forests of northeastern Cambodia, for example, the awarding of state forestry concessions to outside commercial interests led directly to conflicts with local indigenous forest users (see page 32).

Relations, then, between local resource users and state agencies responsible for resource management are often strained and their communications limited. Assumptions about the behaviour and motivation of the other group are often inaccurate. But, in the absence of mechanisms of cooperation, both sides continue to blame the other for resource degradation. Comanagement efforts cannot succeed without a minimum level of communication, collaboration, and trust between local users and governments.

Empowering local resource users through dialogue

In the Philippines, for example, decades of commercial logging reduced forest cover from an estimated 70% of land area in 1900 to 18% a century later. In the 1990s, a logging ban was introduced, and community forestry legislation was approved to encourage alternative livelihoods and responsible use of local forests.

Despite many projects supporting community forestry, few communities ever received formal approvals under the legislation to cut timber. Researchers at the International Institute of Rural Reconstruction (IIRR) undertook action research to build capacity in community forest management. But they had to reconsider their basic assumptions once they secured community participation in the project.

The community felt strongly that the problem was not a lack of forest management knowledge or skills. Nor did they cite dwindling forest resources. Rather, they blamed the problem on the failure of government staff at the national and local levels to implement forestry policies effectively.

Instead of devolving authority for forest management to the local community under provisions of the legislation, government officials were imposing onerous requirements and demanding detailed and costly inventory and management assessments. The communities, who couldn't afford to jump through these bureaucratic hoops, resorted to illegal logging to survive. But they ended up having to pay bribes to local forest protection staff and police to haul their logs to lumber mills. And once delivered, they did not receive fair market prices because they lacked official documentation.

On the one hand, community loggers, cutting timber on their own community forest lands, were paying a steep economic penalty. The state also lost out on the timber royalties and fees that could have been earned from legal logging. On the other hand, the mill owners and some police and forest protection staff benefited personally from the situation.

On the government side, professional foresters argued that communities could not be trusted to manage forestlands effectively. On the community side, loggers complained that officials were lining their own pockets and therefore did not want to honour the original intent of the community forestry policy. Neither side had any direct means of communication with the other. Communities could not get a hearing with senior government staff, and forestry officials had no credibility with communities.

IIRR abandoned their original research strategy and decided to try something altogether different: they brought together senior forestry officials, community representatives, academics, and NGOs in a structured setting, a workshop, to discuss the issues.

With careful preparation, facilitation and management, all parties were given equal opportunity to share their experiences and frustrations without risk of personal attacks.

Many participants were surprised by what they heard. Positions began to shift, and by the end of the 4-day workshop, multistakeholder groups had put together positive recommendations for change. Some of these were quickly adopted in national forest policies and in internal administrative reforms. These innovative tools to facilitate constructive communications between government officials and resource-dependent communities have since been refined and taught by IIRR to other organizations (O'Hara 2006).

> Comanagement efforts cannot succeed without a minimum level of communication, collaboration, and trust between local resource users and governments.

Social equity and the environment

Policies intended to increase commercial use of natural resources often emphasize private resource tenure. Such policies may increase overall investment and earnings from resource exploitation, yet not help the poor. Shrimp ponds and aquaculture enclosures, for example, displace those poor farmers and artisanal fishers who cannot afford such systems (see the Viet Nam case study, page 38). Commercial logging or forest plantation concessions displace traditional shifting cultivation, further impoverishing upland residents who may have no farmland of their own. The ill effects of such resource-management changes are masked by overall increases in production and total income. While some groups benefit, many of the rural poor become even worse off. Commercial resource investments that ignore ecological processes and social equity usually prove unsustainable.

To restate the argument, a resource management system based on individual private tenure is relatively simple. Individuals or corporations with rights to use resources such as land and trees, even if they don't own the resource, can exploit them under agreed terms. This form of resource rights makes it easier for users to respond to commercial markets — which explains why it also figures so prominently in land reform policies. But private tenure is often not appropriate for resource ecosystems such as forests, pastures, and fisheries. These ecosystems are very difficult for individuals to manage. They are also often used as primary or supplemental sources of food and income by poor people, who have limited access to land or other assets. To avoid the pitfalls of open access and resource degradation, or increased conflict, institutions that allow for group management decisions are necessary.

Most attention has focused on governments as agents of collective action or, at the other extreme, of local traditional practices. Government agencies have a mixed record in common pool resource management. Inadequate ecological knowledge and eagerness to promote commercial profits have sometimes led to overexploitation and displacement of the poor. On the other hand, traditional local institutions, which may have long experience with resource management, need to adapt to the growing pressures of human population and more intensive resource exploitation. New arrangements in which local institutions can be facilitated and supported by governments offer an option. Unless new comanagement rights and institutions can be developed, the poor may be squeezed out by commercial and demographic pressures.

Finding the right research approach

Rural poverty and resource degradation in marginal areas are not new problems. While attempts to address them through applied research have attracted lots of attention over the years, results have not often reached large numbers of poor farmers.

Much scientific effort has gone into improved varieties of a small number of food crops. The resulting yield increases have been dramatic and of great benefit to farmers in fertile agricultural areas. But the production cornucopia seen in those well-endowed regions has eluded smallholder farmers in upland and semi-arid zones. This is partly because production conditions there are much more varied and partly because smallholders have such limited land that they must rely on CPRs and other resources, especially livestock. Even if farmers were to enjoy predictable growing conditions and have access to the fertilizer, water, and soils needed by high-yielding varieties, production gains in a single crop might not make much difference to their overall incomes. Only recently have research approaches focused on the management problems of CPRs and their links to agricultural systems (Sayer and Campbell 2004).

One option has been to focus instead on policies that foster conservation and more sustainable resource use. Policy reforms have been proposed for agriculture, forestry, fisheries, and environmental management. However, even when persistent research and advocacy yield major policy changes, these may be insufficient to create lasting change on the ground. The earlier example from the Philippines describes the problems facing poor forest communities after the approval of community forestry policies by the national government. Policy reforms are often difficult to implement or enforce. They may be necessary but, by themselves, are not usually enough to stimulate improvements in the living conditions of the poorest.

Research approaches have evolved in response to lack of progress in reaching the poor. Agricultural scientists increasingly recognize that crops, soils, forests, water, and people are all ecologically linked and that research-based solutions must reflect that integration. Farming systems research, for example, recognized that smallholders adopt multiple agricultural strategies. So leading researchers, by the early 1990s, regularly included new studies of integrated agroecological production techniques, taking into account livestock, crops, trees, and even aquaculture.

More recently, agricultural and NRM researchers have designed and applied modeling tools that factor in biophysical and economic conditions in the study of resource management. But, like farming systems research, even these integrated research strategies neglected many of the social and institutional issues surrounding the use of common pool resources.

Who has access to CPRs? How are decisions about use of collective resources made? And what legitimizes this access? Traditional practices? Modern legal systems? How are resource rights and management adapting in response to changing demographic, economic, social, and ecological trends? What are the links between national policies and local practices that degrade resources? Research that fails to address the dynamic policy, institutional, and social constraints facing resource-dependent rural people may still be able to come up with new production technologies that perform well in test plots. But it will fail to improve the lives of these poor farmers and fishers.

Research that fails to address the dynamic policy, institutional, and social constraints facing resource-dependent rural people may still be able to come up with new production technologies that perform well in test plots. But it will fail to improve the lives of these poor farmers and fishers.

Possibly the most important element missing from traditional empirical research has been poor men and women themselves. Most research ignores or downplays their capacities, knowledge, and judgement. Scientists can be led to believe that years of specialized studies mean they have nothing to learn from poor, illiterate farmers or fishers. The poor are seen as recipients of aid and instruction, unable to find their way out of poverty without expert help. Even the poor themselves come to believe this, as they hear it so often. Poverty has many dimensions, but this lack of recognition for the capacity of the poor to act as agents of their own destinies merely disempowers and impoverishes them further.

Biophysical research, market research, and policy research have provided a broad range of options for poor farmers working under varying conditions. But these efforts typically stop short of recognizing that it is the poor producers themselves, not the researchers, whose learning is most important. The test of an innovation's success is that local resource users adopt and adapt it in their community's fields, forests, or ponds.

A new approach to research was needed — one that would place poor resource users at the centre of the research enterprise as full participants, both teachers and learners. This approach would have to integrate better understanding of natural systems with socially appropriate management interventions selected and tested by local women and men. Further, what was required was a research strategy that could simultaneously strengthen local livelihoods and point to necessary policy change. From 1997 to 2004, IDRC developed and supported a range of research projects, in different regions, that attempted to address these challenges.

In the mid-1990s, participatory action research was still largely unknown in the agricultural research institutes of the developing world. Yet, as an approach to research that had gradually gained scientific credibility and methodological depth in the preceding years, it seemed a promising framework with which to tackle the challenges of natural resource management (Chambers 1989). The specific approaches taken, and aspects emphasized, by IDRC's research programs varied somewhat among regions, reflecting the diversity of development contexts.

In Latin America, the Middle East, and Africa, participatory and interdisciplinary research projects were promoted. But the largest number of projects explicitly adopting a community-based, user-centred framework of participatory action research were in the poor regions of Asia. This is where more than two-thirds of the world's extreme poor live (those earning less than US $1 per day), most of them in rural areas. Many of these research projects focused on common pool resources.

This book reports on a handful of cases that are representative of this participatory action research framework. The research projects had widely differing objectives, contexts, and locations but all focused on ways to improve the management of natural resources for the benefit of local people. In each case, researchers analyzed their experience to draw a range of specific conclusions relevant to the sites and problems with which they were working. Our aim here is not to review all these conclusions, which are presented in detail in research reports and other publications. Instead, we concentrate on describing and comparing comanagement arrangements: how the projects enabled greater local engagement in resource planning and management, and what contributed to their success.

On the Web
THE ISSUE

Part 2

Research for Comanagement

A spectrum of power-sharing options

Comanagement arrangements will vary with the nature of the resource, the political context, the expertise and skills of participating organizations, and the degree of mutual trust. Most analysts agree there is a broad spectrum of comanagement arrangements (Figure 2). At one end, authority for NRM remains with the state, but local communities are consulted on specific issues. At the other end of the spectrum are arrangements that give communities or resource user groups broad authority to take management decisions, but require them to report periodically to the responsible state agency.

This picture is complicated further because of the range of management decisions that may be involved, from policymaking and planning, to setting rules, allocating harvests, investing in resource productivity, monitoring and enforcement, determining membership in user groups, and adjudicating conflicts. Some of these management actions may involve multiple actors other than the local resource users and governments. These could be private corporations with a stake in resource development or conservation organizations or NGOs representing external interests in the protection of local resources.

Figure 2. Spectrum of resource comanagement arrangements (adapted from Goetze 2004).

Neighbouring communities, too, may be represented in comanagement arrangements. This is because resource use and management practices in one location often influence other communities through larger scale landscape and ecosystem linkages. Upstream diversion of water for irrigation, for example, may have serious consequences downstream. The interests of these peripheral communities may be represented either directly or through government.

In the Kenyan highlands, as traditional pastoral livelihoods gave way to mixed farming, land that had been managed communally was allocated to farmers. However, farming communities soon found that the well-being of their livestock and crops depended on common resources: water supplies, bushlands, and shared pastures. Private landowners voluntarily organized new NRM associations that engaged neighbouring communities in landscape-scale resource management consultations.

Of course, various agencies and levels of government with expertise in, or jurisdiction over, a particular resource will normally be represented in a comanagement scheme. In the case of Viet Nam's lagoon fisheries, comanagement arrangements involved local village leaders, as the main initiative was at the municipal level (the commune). However, district government officials responsible for fisheries management were key players in implementation and coordination with neighbouring municipalities. The support of senior provincial technical staff was essential as well (see page 38).

There are two broad conceptual approaches to comanagement. One is premised on formal agreement between all the parties on detailed rights, responsibilities, and procedures in relation to the various resources in question. Negotiations focus on the details of power sharing and governance. This approach has been typical of the comanagement agreements adopted in Canada, for example, between First Nations and provincial and federal governments (Goetze 2004). Issues of jurisdiction and legal authority were more pressing than environmental degradation.

The second approach is to gear comanagement arrangements to meeting urgent functional needs of the ecosystem and resource users. The starting point is consideration of specific environmental and livelihood problems in need of resolution and of different stakeholders' interests. With this approach, various parties are brought together to design management strategies to address their problems. The details of power sharing and structure are an outcome of processes of action and learning, not the central focus of intervention. This approach is sometimes referred to as adaptive comanagement (Carlsson and Berkes, 2005).

For example, in the case of Bhutan (see page 49), the driving force behind a new water management scheme was the shortages experienced by downstream communities whose rice crops were threatened. Ecological and livelihood pressures drove the parties involved to a practical solution that met all users' needs — and more equitably. The resolution was aided by policy reform, but did not rely on new legal agreements.

The six research cases discussed in this book emphasize the second approach. The comanagement structures that emerged with the help of research were not derived from legal negotiations over governance. Rather, they arose from learning to make resource use more productive, more sustainable, and more equitable. The cases do not examine resource use from the point of view of government, although its role is often very important. The formal technical roles of public-sector NRM agencies have been thoroughly studied elsewhere, and there are many international models for their application.

The focus of these six cases, then, is on the community end of the comanagement partnership. Community groups typically lack the political influence of governments and private commercial investors. Yet the experience of numerous resource management failures suggests that the local level is where resource management initiatives unravel.

Local people bring both knowledge and rights to resource management decision-making. Ignoring these strengths often incurs high environmental and social costs; so it is imperative to find ways to recognize, harness, and reinforce local capacity for resource-related decision-making. The project cases focus on innovations that build local capacity, institutions, and livelihoods through effective natural resource comanagement. They provide lessons for practitioners to address these needs in the field.

Beyond theory: action-oriented research

The research programs supported by IDRC adopted several distinctive features in response to this backdrop of context-specific relationships and stakeholder capacities. Of course, the thematic focus of the research was natural resource management. That meant the developing-country researchers had to not only examine the natural ecosystems and trends in their productivity but also develop practical local interventions to reduce resource degradation. The research, then, was not about abstract hypothesis testing; it was about achieving results, about strengthening the livelihoods of the poor. It was recognized at the outset that innovations aimed solely at conserving resources, that is, without building family and community assets or opening up income opportunities, would not likely be adopted by poor farmers and fishers.

Despite the vast differences in cultures, production systems, biophysical constraints, and policies across different countries and sites, the research experience tended to unfold in an analogous fashion everywhere. There were several common elements.

Developing new methodologies

Local researchers were enthusiastic about new approaches to thorny local problems. But they were also apprehensive. Although participatory methods had prominent promoters in academic and development circles in the 1990s, they were new to many of the developing-country scientists working on IDRC-funded projects. In many countries, these methods were not being widely taught. Interdisciplinary approaches were also something of a novelty. Researchers were accustomed to conducting studies in their own areas of expertise, not organizing joint fieldwork with experts in other disciplines.

The first step in these NRM research projects was therefore to identify and explore new methodologies. Training in participatory research tools and multidisciplinary explorations of field issues jointly with local men and women helped expand researchers' horizons. And, given the natural sciences background of many agricultural researchers working on these projects, a special effort was made to tap social science contributions to NRM. But it was also apparent that the conventional practices of individual disciplines were insufficient, that new interdisciplinary tools had to be developed for specific needs.

This research agenda would be challenging in any environment. In the remote field sites of developing countries, often marked by conflict and deprivation, it was unrealistic to expect local research organizations with modest resources to start off with state-of-the-art research methods. Part of the intent of the IDRC approach, then, was to build the capacity of partner organizations — both to tackle immediate problems and to deal with longer term issues. While training and methodology development were important, the accent was put on action learning, or "learning by doing."

Learning by doing: the interplay of urgency and caution

Local people in the research sites typically faced urgent problems. On the one hand, they could not wait for lengthy analyses or accommodate the academic schedules of distant organizations before taking action. On the other, they couldn't afford the costs of failed experiments. Researchers were uncertain about the probable outcomes of recommended interventions and favoured a conservative approach. At each site and project, collaboration between resource users and researchers resulted in a unique interplay of these forces of urgency and caution.

Immediate problems stimulated researchers to press their agenda more actively. And the resources of the research projects (expertise and funds) helped reduce the risk to local farmers and fishers who might otherwise be reluctant to test innovations. Early interventions that addressed urgent local problems demonstrated the responsiveness of researchers and their commitment to obtaining meaningful local input into the research agenda. They built trust, enhancing the researchers' reputations. Addressing urgent resource constraints strengthened the position of poor resource users, allowing them to increase productivity and generate a surplus that allowed further experimentation.

The types of interventions expected of the research varied with the local context. They could be technical efforts to improve resource productivity by introducing new agriculture, agroforestry, aquaculture, livestock, or integrated production systems. Or they might be the design and creation of new institutions to resolve conflicts or secure collective tenure. In marginal agroecosystems, where CPRs are essential to the livelihoods of the poor, both kinds of innovations are generally needed. Hence, the question of where to start was largely a pragmatic one. For innovations to be adopted and adapted by the resource users themselves, they had to be practical, sensible, and understandable. They had to be tested and validated by the farmers and fishers themselves.

Long-term fieldwork provided the real proof of the NRM research framework. The research was premised on shared learning between researchers and resource users, each group benefiting from the other's experience. This was time-consuming: it involved joint diagnosis, analysis, exploration, intervention, and evaluation. It required strengthening local organizations for collective action

> Long-term fieldwork provided the real proof of the NRM research framework. The research was premised on shared learning between researchers and resource users, each group benefiting from the other's experience.

to address poverty. This step of experience sharing was essential, however, not only for consolidating lessons from the field research, but also for building adaptive learning skills in the community itself.

Learning how to learn together

The experience with this NRM research suggested that expert-generated solutions were ineffective in addressing complex human–ecosystem interactions. To come up with appropriate alternatives, all project participants — researchers, government officials, and local resource users — had to adopt new attitudes toward knowledge and learning.

Researchers are taught that their advanced studies make them experts, the people with the solutions. So learning from local people with little formal education but much expertise required them to change their attitudes and find ways to validate such local learning scientifically. For their part, local people who selected strategies for implementation needed ways to test and document their experience more formally. And both the researchers and local people had to learn to communicate lessons to government officials and other outsiders. These were unfamiliar processes for all participants, requiring much discussion and experimentation.

The recognition of and respect for local knowledge meant that learning became much more explicitly social. Researchers and farmers had to learn how to move between two different frames of understanding: the cumulative empirical knowledge of modern science and the contextual knowledge created, applied, and passed on by women and men through daily life.

The researchers also had to acknowledge from the outset that communities are ill-defined and heterogeneous. Interests diverge, wealth and power separate, social relations are complex and dynamic, and histories matter. Gender analysis is essential to identify the varying impacts of resource degradation and management interventions for women, a group often excluded from resource use decisions and benefits. Differences of culture, ethnicity, and language can make these factors opaque to outsiders, whether from the other side of the river or the other side

> Gender analysis is essential to identify the varying impacts of resource degradation and management interventions for women, a group often excluded from resource use decisions and benefits.

of the planet. Local situations are each a bit different and easily misinterpreted if researchers arrive with a fixed agenda.

Local leadership

Many of the concepts and research methods applied in these cases were elaborated from work pioneered in international research centres and northern universities. But the projects described here were led by local researchers. It took considerable courage, creativity, and persistence for them to introduce new methods and attitudes to their research organizations and field partners.

For example, one starting point was to investigate the structure of rights surrounding access to resources. Lack of formal rights, conflict over rights, or loss of long-standing resource rights all undermine users' ability to manage the resource base and lead to degradation. Understanding these rights and the institutions through which they are contested was a prerequisite for effective intervention and change. Researchers could not escape involvement in politically charged local conflicts and took real professional risks when the conventional wisdom argued against these approaches.

Local leadership also meant that researchers had to engage local governments and resource users in the research from the start. The recognition that local women and men would be the chief agents of learning and change meant that local initiative, and local government support for such initiative, should be fostered through the research.

Outreach for change

The research teams found that once their projects were delivering results, it was not enough for them just to return to their offices and write academic papers. Many research outcomes pointed to the need for changes in resource rights and policy to ensure that benefits would reach poor local resource users. Sharing these results and working to ensure practical changes were implemented required time and effort. The researchers connected with NGOs, government agencies, other researchers, and sometimes with international donors to document and share their findings. They helped advocacy groups to understand and make use of the evidence from their work. And they helped local communities to link with other communities and with senior government officials so that their voices could be more clearly heard.

The participatory nature of the research, then, was tightly linked to recognition of poor farmers and fishers as the most important agents of change and development, and not merely targets of technological advice. The emphasis on indigenous knowledge, on understanding institutions, and on practical and sustainable interventions all made it imperative for the researchers and local people to be jointly engaged in learning. The resulting lessons had to be convincing for poor farmers or fishers to risk investing in innovations. The best evidence would end up coming from the users themselves.

Part 3

Experiences from the Field

On the Web
THE RESEARCH

The six brief case studies that follow present a cross-section of research projects supported by IDRC that reveal lessons for comanagement. These are real stories about real people — from Asia, Latin America, and the Middle East, where researchers and rural people learned together how to put theory into practice to improve lives and livelihoods. The projects were selected to cover a wide range of contexts, climates, political systems, and cultures, from one of the largest countries in the world to some of the smallest. The research underlying these projects took place over a number of years, sometimes through several multiyear funding phases. More details on these and many other IDRC-supported projects can be found at www.idrc.ca/in_focus_comanagement.

The research was carried out in each case by teams combining multiple disciplines. They were based in national research centres or universities, and sometimes they were led by NGOs or by government agencies. But in every case it was the rural people themselves who became the real leaders, as they responded to an approach that — often for the first time — took account of their local knowledge and experience. The consistency of that response in a diversity of situations illustrates the broad applicability of the approach in marginal areas where poor people depend on common pool resources (CPRs).

CAMBODIA: resource conflicts and community tenure

Documenting traditional local use and management of forests was new territory for both researchers and villagers.

Key features of the research

Methodology: indigenous knowledge, participatory mapping, nonformal education

Rights: traditional resource rights secured

Governance: participatory planning, natural resource management committees

Partnerships and networks: strong links to provincial government departments, national program, the United Nations Development Programme (UNDP), NGOS

Policy: land tenure reforms

What price prosperity?

Civil war brought Cambodia years of chaos, devastation, and anarchy, and the unforgettable images of the killing fields. Now, in a time of relative peace, Cambodian society has regained a large measure of stability and even prosperity. One of the sources of that prosperity is the heavily forested uplands of the northeastern province of Ratanakiri (Figure 3). Encouraged by the central government, investors and migrant workers have moved into the province in search of resource wealth.

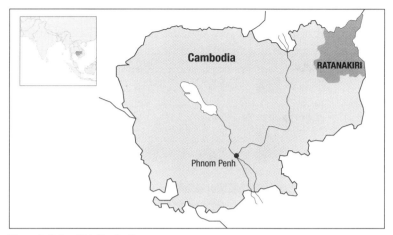

Figure 3. Ratanakiri, Cambodia.

Unfortunately, that wealth often comes at a high price for the hill people of Ratanakiri. Belonging to nine different ethnic minority groups, they make up over two-thirds of the area's population and practice shifting cultivation. For the most part, they share neither language nor religious beliefs with the dominant lowland Khmer people, who are rice growers and regard the hill people as "backward."

As the central government readily awarded forest and plantation concessions in a bid to boost investment, lowlanders migrated to the province. But the forest was already used extensively by the local people — as a source of food, medicine, building materials, and water, and for the cultivation of upland rice in a rotational management system led by village elders. Now they found that, without any consultation, armed men hired by concession holders were cutting the forests they had used for generations.

As one villager described it: "They just came here to look for workers to clear the land. Some of the supervisors were good but some were fierce and carried guns. They use guns to intimidate the people." Another said they were told their cows, which traditionally were allowed to roam freely in search of forage, would be shot if they wandered into concession areas.

Not surprisingly there were conflicts over land and resources. The provincial government in Ratanakiri was concerned. But it had no control over the awarding of concessions by the national government in Phnom Penh and knew very little about the ethnic minority communities. At the same time, international and local NGOs were questioning the fairness of the government's actions and the outcomes of change in Ratanakiri.

With support from IDRC and the blessing of the provincial government, a research team was formed to explore how the problems of poverty and resource conflicts could be addressed at the local level. They began by working with local villagers to learn about the situation they faced. That situation was summed up by Seu Chil, a woman farmer: "We are highlanders. Our lives depend on the forests and the land. Without forests and land we cannot live. We need firewood, vegetables, fruits, mushrooms, and bamboo shoots from the forests. We see the forests as our market."

"We are highlanders. Our lives depend on the forests and the land. Without forests and land we cannot live."

The research team had experience in agriculture, forestry, and natural sciences. But they realized early on that education and awareness building were needed to help local people recognize their legal rights. Also that local people needed evidence of their long history of resource use and management to legitimize their claims. This was new territory both for the researchers and the villagers.

Establishing a precedent

Using participatory appraisal and mapping techniques, and relying on the knowledge and authority of elders, the researchers helped villagers to prepare detailed plans of their traditional territory and its use. The research team sought social science skills to apply these participatory methods. The next step was to develop rules for resource allocation within these territories based on customary practices. The maps and proposed rules were then discussed with the commune (municipal) government. Neighbouring villages were also given an opportunity to comment. Once district officials had given their endorsement, the plans were submitted to provincial authorities, and finally the governor of Ratanakiri was asked to approve the plans.

When the governor approved the first of these community plans in 2000, the concessionaire in conflict with the community was obliged to withdraw its claim to most of the community's forest area. This established a precedent. The legitimacy of well-documented traditional resource rights made these rights a valid subject of government attention. And it gave government departments and local development NGOs a model of how they could be secured.

This process of participatory land use planning emerged through experimentation and fieldwork involving local communities and government agencies, not from any formal policy prescriptions. The maps and documentary evidence were important in changing the assumptions of all the participants. Government officials, who were not familiar with local languages and cultures, were surprised to learn that forest resources were extensively used and managed by local communities. And the villagers came to recognize that there were limits to their use of the land in the face of external claims.

> Government officials were surprised to learn that forest resources were extensively used and managed by local communities.

Government staff had as much to learn as local people. The research project was structured to engage government staff in learning, not to confront them with local activism. Their traditional role had been to enforce the administrative regulations of the central government, a role in which they were often obliged to oppose local communities. The research project provided a mechanism for provincial staff in Ratanakiri to experiment with new professional behaviours: consultation, respect for the rights of citizens, facilitation of local initiatives, and responsiveness to local problems.

These local planning processes became quite effective in resolving conflicts and in building the capacity of new local and provincial government structures. The early successes attracted the attention of many other communities, and the research team sponsored several innovative measures to disseminate research results and to build local capacity. These included informal classes to build the Khmer language and numeracy skills of the villagers, as well as farmer-to-farmer and village-to-village exchange visits.

A model for the nation

Soon the newly empowered communities began to form natural resource management committees to help map and negotiate resource use and to implement local management plans. They also ensured that natural resource issues were included in mandatory commune development plans. Provincial government departments retained responsibility for training, oversight, and coordination, as well as for managing any conflict and supporting enforcement of the local plans.

The research team identified the need to improve agricultural production systems in ethnic minority communities. But they were unable to devote as much attention to this part of their work as they hoped because the question of tenure security still had not been adequately resolved, and this remained the most pressing issue for the communities themselves.

Despite these important local gains, community tenure and planning processes were not enshrined in national legislation. Researchers recognized that the drafting of a new Land Law then underway provided an opportunity to address the issue. By networking extensively with provincial and national governments, NGOs, and other development actors, the research team was able to demonstrate the importance of this issue in the context of Ratanakiri and contribute to successful efforts by many groups to have community land tenure included in the final legislation.

Early in the project the research team made a strategic decision to align field research activities with a large UNDP-led service delivery project in the region. One result was that the participatory natural resource planning process developed in Ratanakiri was incorporated within a new nation-wide local governance reform program supported by UNDP. A senior member of the research team was hired by UNDP to lead the adaptation of the land-use planning tool for use by local governments throughout the country. A similar process was also adopted by the Ministry of Land as the mechanism for extending land titling and registry throughout Cambodia.

Resource management in Ratanakiri continues to present challenges. Implementation of policy reforms has led to disputes over which government agency should be responsible for the new local management processes. As well, improved access to the province is increasing market-related pressure on resources. But with strengthened capacities and effective models for intervention, local resource users, local governments, and provincial agencies all have better tools to take on the political and practical issues that development will inevitably bring.

VIET NAM: sharing the resource in Tam Giang Lagoon

Science-based comanagement helped local fishers and other users to formulate plans for sharing the wealth of this biologically productive waterway.

Key features of the research

Methodology: multistakeholder participatory resource planning and management

Livelihoods: agricultural and aquacultural technologies for low-income households

Rights: recognition of customary rights and access to resources

Governance: new participatory and representative processes for local government

Partnerships and networks: strong links to local and provincial governments

Policy: tested implementation of new national fisheries comanagement policy

A unique resource

Although the coast of neighbouring Viet Nam is not far from the Cambodian highlands, the setting is very different. So are the resources at stake. Here, too, lack of participatory planning and management brought the threat of violent conflict and serious damage to a valuable resource. And, as in Cambodia, the engagement of resource users and government in the research process helped point to new options for action.

Viet Nam's unique Tam Giang – Cau Hai Lagoon system is over 70 km long (Figure 4), but averages only 2 m in depth. The lagoon is a highly productive habitat for both freshwater and marine species, and has long been an important fishery. Most of the more than 300 000 people living on the margins of the lagoon depend on fishing or farming for their livelihoods.

In 1995, IDRC and the Canadian International Development Agency (CIDA) funded a study of the condition of the aquatic resource base and its use by communities around the lagoon. The research team brought together for the first time agricultural

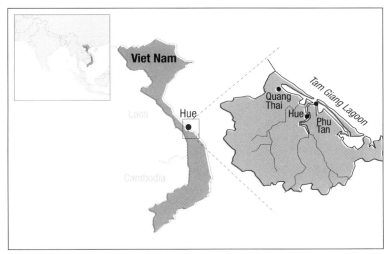

Figure 4. Tam Giang Lagoon, Viet Nam.

scientists from Hue University of Agriculture and Forestry (HUAF), biologists and sociologists from Hue University of Sciences, and administrators from the provincial department of fisheries. This led to an unusual degree of collaboration among scientists from a variety of disciplines and government officials. "It provided us with a new model of how to collaborate effectively with government agencies," comments HUAF's rector, Tran Van Minh.

Working at three sites in different parts of the lagoon, the multidisciplinary team soon discovered that, although the government had introduced reforms for agricultural land, it had not considered aquatic resource tenure. Prime fishing areas in the lagoon were held by families on the basis of local custom. They had invested in permanent fishing structures such as fish corrals that took advantage of the currents to guide fish into narrow traps or nets.

The poorest members of each community were the mobile fishers, who had no land holdings and lived with their families on their boats. Because of the difficulty of delivering basic services such as education and health care, the government encouraged them to settle in existing communities on the margins of the lagoon. One such community was in Quang Thai commune at the northern end of the lagoon. Here they struggled to fish alongside established neighbours who had the benefit of access to agricultural land as well.

In an effort to reduce pressure on the lagoon and strengthen livelihoods, the researchers first introduced a new cash crop, peanuts, which thrived in the sandy soil. This early success built community confidence and soon was adopted by neighbouring villages. The researchers then turned their attention to the more difficult challenges of the aquatic resource base. They helped poor fishers assess the resource habitat and identify areas for restricting fishing and protecting against illegal fishing methods. The researchers also introduced simple cage aquaculture based on feeding the fish local sea grass. Aquaculture was an appealing option, in part to boost the income of women who lacked access to the most productive fishing grounds and gear.

Early success built community confidence and was adopted by neighbouring villages.

Unplanned growth

Meanwhile, in the more productive central lagoon commune of Phu Tan, work with the communities and local government focused on the spread of small-scale shrimp ponds and net enclosures. At the beginning of the 1990s, such enclosures were virtually unknown in the lagoon waters, but by the end of the decade they covered 75% of the commune's water territory. Shrimp ponds built out from flooded rice fields on the low-lying shore occupied another 20% of the water surface. There was hardly any open water left!

Despite the lack of regulations, all levels of government encouraged this rapid unplanned growth. Local government earned fees from formalizing newly claimed private tenures, while provincial and national governments earned higher taxes and national export revenues from the high-value products. But the aquaculture boom created problems. Water quality and current flow declined dramatically, creating conditions for disease and reducing productivity. The increased privatization of the common pool resources of the lagoon hit the poorest fishers hard, forcing them to try fishing in other territories that were already heavily exploited.

> "No one actually manages and takes responsibility for what happens there. All the different organizations want to have rights, but that is all."

The issue that finally attracted government attention was the loss of waterways through the maze of net enclosures. In the words of Nguyen Luong Hien, director of the provincial fisheries department: "Everybody acknowledges how important the lagoon is. However, no one actually manages and takes responsibility for what happens there. All the different organizations want to have rights, but that is all."

The researchers worked with local government, with the net enclosure owners, and with mobile gear fishers, who hoped the reopening of waterways would allow them greater local fishing opportunities. Through participatory mapping, examination of water quality data, and negotiation with the different interests, the research team facilitated the design of appropriate clearings for navigation and water exchange. However, disagreement between mobile fishers and net enclosure owners stalled agreement on fishing rights in waters adjacent to net enclosures. Interestingly, researchers observed that women were able to negotiate better terms for fishing access than men, because they were perceived to use less aggressive fishing techniques.

An impatient local government — without consulting the researchers — implemented the waterway plan, and police forced net enclosure owners to relocate their operations. The local government adopted neither the conflict resolution measures nor the

On the Web
THE RESEARCH

provisions for shared fishing access in the waterways that had been proposed by the research team. Negotiations collapsed and conflicts between mobile gear fishers and net enclosure owners escalated into violence.

A radically different approach

This experience brought home to provincial fisheries officials the arguments of the research team that conventional top-down planning would not work. Eventually, they were willing to consider a radically different approach in Quang Thai commune, where conflicts were now emerging as fish pens proliferated. The research team made it clear that solutions could come only from participatory planning and comanagement, in which local fishers and governments agreed on guiding principles for use of the resources and made commitments that could be jointly enforced. They were aided by the introduction in 2003 of new national legislation providing for fisheries comanagement through locally defined user groups, and specifically mandating provincial authorities to implement the legislation.

All the parties involved could now benefit from the experience gained in 6 years of participatory research:

➤ The provincial department of fisheries saw this as an opportunity to solve an obvious problem and test practical implementation strategies for its new mandate.

➤ Local fishers had learned a lot about the lagoon resource base, and had sufficient information to make reasoned arguments and plans.

➤ The research team had acquired skills in communications and facilitation and could lead the process without imposing solutions.

With strong motivation and an untested new policy mandate, fishers in Quang Thai proposed forming a user group. Its first

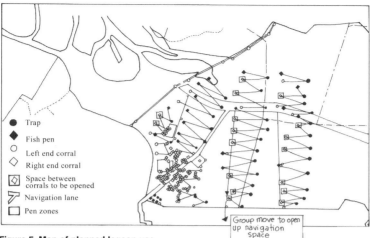

Legend:
- ● Trap
- ◆ Fish pen
- ○ Left end corral
- ◇ Right end corral
- ▨ Space between corrals to be opened
- ⟆ Navigation lane
- ▭ Pen zones

Group move to open up navigation space

Figure 5. Map of planned lagoon use.

task would be to formulate a plan for allocation of the lagoon's surface area (Figure 5).

The lagoon planning process was launched at a stakeholder meeting and workshop. The research team provided technical resources and facilitated consensus on key problems and overall strategy for the planning process. All participants agreed that the plan should maintain access for all current users, respect customary rights, and share the dislocations needed to re-arrange gear in the lagoon waters.

The plan took shape through application of participatory research and shared information from joint mapping, focus group surveys, and group analysis. The process reinforced local knowledge as well as the insights from scientific research, and provided a foundation for new approaches to comanagement and local governance. Researchers used participatory mapping tools to support the new lagoon user group in an analysis of shared responsibilities. Local government officials initiated and led local resource planning. Provincial and district staff provided technical resources and facilitated local conflict management and problem solving.

Now the Quang Thai experience is being replicated in adjoining municipalities in the lagoon. Training materials and guidelines are being developed for provincial staff, who are taking leadership in fostering the new comanagement system. Says the fisheries department's Nguyen Luong Hien: "Now we are looking for ways to better integrate community management and provincial government planning."

ECUADOR: water conflicts and conservation in an Andean watershed

Research data helped break down local misconceptions about water flows and who was consuming more than their fair share.

Key features of the research

Methodology: participatory water monitoring, ecosystem services compensation

Rights: access to water, communal land tenure

Governance: multistakeholder consultative roundtable, collaborative platforms for water users and local governments

Partnerships and networks: links to local NGOs, national government agencies, researchers, and donors

Policy: demonstrating collaborative alternative to private water rights

Conserving a rare ecosystem

Whether you fish or farm, water is essential to your livelihood. In the mountain valleys of the El Angel watershed in northeastern Ecuador (Figure 6), marginal farmers find their livelihoods at risk because they never know from one day to the next whether they will have enough water for their fields and homes. Their farms are downstream of the main water source and, although the government issues water licenses to regulate withdrawals from streams and rivers, those who live downstream don't always get their fair share.

Figure 6. El Angel watershed, Carchi Province, Ecuador.

The watershed's elevation ranges from 1 500 to 4 000 m. At the top is a wetland plateau that forms the El Angel Ecological Reserve. The cold high-altitude wetlands are unique. They soak up rainfall like a sponge and release it to the rest of the watershed slowly through the year. Most of the plant species here are found only in these fragile and cold tropical wetlands. The cloud forests adjacent to the wetlands are among the rarest ecosystems in the Andes. There is also great potential for ecotourism, but the forests are threatened by agricultural expansion.

Many of the irrigation canals serving farmers lower in the valley originate here. The area of influence of the El Angel River includes a large peripheral zone in the lower reaches of the watershed, irrigated by water drawn from the river high upstream.

In 1996, a team of natural and social scientists supported by IDRC found that the problems are in part due to climatic variation with altitude, but are compounded by issues of land and water access rights. Private landholdings vary widely, from large haciendas to very small properties carved out by peasants during various land reforms. But there are also communal territories of indigenous peoples who still occupy ancestral lands. Many of these are in the wetlands, overlapping the Ecological Reserve, and in the zones in which irrigation canals originate.

Taking a bit more

At the other extreme, the low-lying valleys are semi-arid and hot, with shallow, stony soils except in the valley bottoms where farmers grow tropical crops. Unfortunately, they depend entirely on the irrigation water from higher up. As Saloman Acosta, a farmer from this region, complains: "The water coming into our village is totally contaminated ... and there is practically no water during the dry season."

Even though water availability, water quality, and land use were closely linked throughout the watershed, most residents saw only their own local issues. Upstream users believed downstream users were already getting more than their allotted share of water, so they could justify taking a bit more themselves. Sometimes they took a lot more, installing pumps or pipes to draw water illegally into their own fields.

There is a formal system for water allocation covered by national legislation. However, neither stream flow nor withdrawals are measured in any reliable way, and the canals are earth-lined, leaky, and very long. So while the state's records show that the total water concessions in El Angel are still less than the available flow, downstream users sometimes have no water at all for several weeks. Farmer Miguel Angel Cuaspud voices the frustration of many when he says: "The government granted me a right to use water 3 years ago, but it is water that does not exist."

"The government granted me a right to use water 3 years ago, but it is water that does not exist."

Water user associations manage the irrigation systems, and a state-employed water adjudicator processes formal applications for water withdrawals. But without reliable data on which to base judgements, it is impossible to satisfy users. And when their sense of injustice grows, so does water theft. The situation led to increasing and sometimes violent conflict.

Innovative information sharing

To better understand the system and its problems the researchers in the Manrecur project needed an integrated assessment of the entire watershed, its hydrology, and resources, which could be analyzed using geographic information systems (GIS) technology. This led to an important innovation in information sharing: the Carchi Consortium, which was started by the researchers as a way to share data and initiate collaboration on the El Angel watershed with government officials and other organizations active in the watershed.

Informal meetings of the Consortium soon attracted the attention of local communities. Water user associations became involved. Agricultural groups, county governments, and officials from central ministries all were brought in to help clarify the resource situation for the watershed, using the base data generated by the research team. The Consortium has met regularly for 10 years now, attracting farmers, government officials, students, researchers, and others, depending on the issue. The Consortium is an open, nonhierarchical forum. Technical advisors undertake research and respond to questions that arise.

The researchers also devised a simple water flow meter that could be built and used locally. With regular participatory monitoring of key points in the irrigation network, they built up a much better picture of actual flows and uses. Soon the water adjudicator began to make use of the evidence collected by the research team. Applications for more water extraction were refused on the grounds that existing flows were inadequate. Finally, the people of the watershed were forced to realize that their livelihoods were inextricably bound together by the flows of water through the slender canals.

On the Web
THE RESEARCH

In one case, the new data showed that an upstream municipality was withdrawing more water than allowed by its formal concession. The population of the municipality had grown, as had its water needs. Working together with the downstream municipality affected by these water withdrawals, a joint solution was found: both municipalities invested in rehabilitation of an old reservoir. The joint action and the increased awareness of downstream impacts by the upstream municipality meant that water use would be more carefully monitored in future.

Need for participation

Water quality was also a major issue in the El Angel watershed. Most communities use water directly from the canals for domestic purposes and watering livestock, even though it has been contaminated by human and animal waste and by agricultural chemicals upstream. From the wetlands to the valley bottom, the systems of water extraction, agricultural production, chemical use, or livestock management were intrinsically linked to how communities found drinking water or disposed of their wastes. Upstream communities bore a large responsibility for the fate of those downstream. This issue especially engaged women, who assume responsibility for providing domestic water.

The need for user participation, and the engagement of local government in new multistakeholder governance institutions, accompanied a shift in leadership of the research to a new NGO, Grupo Randi Randi. Founded and led by Manrecur project researchers active in El Angel and the Carchi Consortium, this group promoted participatory approaches to resource governance in the watershed. They succeeded in finding support to establish a permanent research station in the wetlands to strengthen knowledge of the ecology and hydrology of that crucial link in the watershed system.

By organizing collection of water flow and quality data by local people, and building on their knowledge, the Manrecur project demonstrated to community organizations the value of evidence in decision making. Researchers used new information-sharing and collaboration techniques to challenge assumptions that were preventing collective action. They demonstrated how this knowledge could be used to negotiate creative solutions to water conflicts and better govern the resource by combining research on hydrology and ecosystem function with practical social science.

Perhaps most important, the researchers highlighted the interconnectedness of the ecosystem's components. Local people have begun to see themselves as inhabitants not just of a particular community but of a watershed. Now they increasingly accept responsibility for its well-being and recognize that the future of the watershed is tied to the health of the wetlands and to joint management of the land and resources.

On the Web
THE RESEARCH

BHUTAN: watershed management and policy reforms

Using participatory methods, researchers helped improve local productivity by integrating their work on crops, livestock, forests, and water resources.

Key features of the research

Methodology: conflict management, role-playing, integrated participatory NRM

Livelihoods: rice production

Rights: access to water

Governance: new watershed management institutions, new relations with local government

Partnerships and networks: links to other research centres and line agencies, project funding shared with the Swiss Agency for Development and Cooperation (SDC)

Policy: water resources management policy, national policy on community-based natural resource management

First come, first served

The Kingdom of Bhutan is a land-locked country of deep valleys and towering mountains. Farmers in the bottom of those valleys, just like farmers in Ecuador's El Angel watershed, often suffered from lack of water. But there was nothing they could do — legally. If the farmers in villages upstream used all the water to irrigate their crops, that was simply your misfortune. "First come, first served" was the traditional way to allocate water, and even aggrieved farmers who resorted to the courts usually found that judges were reluctant to go against tradition.

This was the situation in the Lingmutey Chu watershed (Figure 7), a typical small agricultural valley close to the Renewable Natural Resources Research Centre (RNRRC) at Bajo. Seven small villages dot the sides of the valley; the highest sits at 2 170 m, almost 900 m above its lowest neighbour. Poverty and low agricultural productivity were common, and the scientists at the research centre had worked with the farmers of Lingmutey Chu for some years, endeavouring to strengthen livelihoods and improve resource management.

Originally, RNRRC emphasized conventional in-house research on agricultural commodity production. This achieved some success

Figure 7. Lingmutey Chu watershed, Bhutan.

in developing improved rice varieties and management techniques. But the researchers recognized that constraints to agricultural production have complex and interrelated causes linked to other resource systems and to socioeconomic factors. With support from IDRC and the Swiss Agency for Development and Cooperation (SDC), the researchers adopted a new approach that involved on-farm research on farming systems and resource management in complex mountain ecosystems.

In Lingmutey Chu, the research team developed an integrated, multisectoral research approach to link crops, livestock, forests, and water to improve overall productivity. The research team comprised specialists from a variety of natural science disciplines. Their initial goal was to build relationships between farmers, researchers, and extension workers to extend the scope and impact of research innovations. They shared results with local people to confirm their emerging understanding of resource interactions and conflicts.

On the Web
THE RESEARCH

These participatory research methods were as new to the researchers as they were to the local people, but the villagers quickly became enthusiastic. Commented 68-year-old farmer Ap Wangda: "Never in my life was I consulted ... I was always asked to do. This is the first time that people are asking my views on our needs."

Based on their consultations with the valley people, the researchers undertook specialized studies of selected topics. Technical interventions in production systems arose either from the on-station experiments of the researchers or from the experience of local farmers. But most of the successful interventions were suggested by community members themselves.

> **Most of the successful interventions were suggested by community members themselves.**

The most contentious issue in the watershed, however, was water management for irrigation. The expansion of rice production in the lower watershed created a greater demand for irrigation water during transplanting, just before the June rains when water flows are lowest. Shortages were common. (Bhutan has a monsoon climate, with heavy rains in the months from June to August.)

Changes to the rice cultivation system using late-maturing varieties or low-water irrigation techniques were technically feasible, but none of them was practical. Furthermore, extensive studies of hydrology in the Lingmutey Chu River showed that overall water flows were sufficient for transplanting, but that water was not getting to where it was needed, when it was needed. The research team realized the main problem lay in the traditional water rights system that allocated user rights exclusively to upstream communities.

Half the water was wasted

With no incentive to use water efficiently, the upstream villages took advantage of their "first come, first served" rights and extracted more water than they needed. Over half the water was wasted in inefficient supply canals. The issue was controversial because upstream villages did not want any change in the status quo, but the situation was plainly inequitable. How to overcome tradition?

First, the research team used their hydrological studies to convince users that there was sufficient water for all. Then they introduced role-playing games to help build communication and empathy among the various water user groups. Eventually, the researchers were able to help users negotiate a settlement to introduce a more equitable water-sharing arrangement. This required the formation of a basin-wide consultation forum and development of permanent mechanisms for resolving water allocation disputes.

The example of Lingmutey Chu was by no means unique; in fact, it illustrated a broader problem throughout Bhutan, where water disputes have been common. The government adopted the lessons from Lingmutey Chu and endorsed the principles of equitable access to water resources. This policy change, which took place as the local dispute was still being negotiated, helped to convince the local parties of the need to accept changes. The new policy provides for mechanisms by which downstream users can compensate those upstream who, because of improved management, can release more water.

The researchers learned the importance of policy in helping to address integrated resource management issues. The new national policy provided local officials and villagers with guidance on how they should resolve these issues. The example of the consultative watershed forum developed in Lingmutey Chu served as a precedent for implementing the new policy.

Overcoming challenges

A similar approach to collective action was applied in the case of community forestry in Lingmutey Chu, but with mixed success. The formation of community forest user groups and management committees in several villages led to the establishment of community-managed plantations of complex forests. The objective of ensuring access to all proved difficult to sustain, however. Some of the poorer villagers, especially women heads of households, could not always contribute fully to maintaining the plantations, and came into conflict with other user group members. Wealthier farmers and larger landowners began to dominate decision-making. Some of the women have since dropped out of management committees.

This provided a clear demonstration of how challenging it can be to build equitable resource management institutions in the face of deeply imbedded social and political inequities. But there is ample evidence that the new collective resource management institutions in Lingmutey Chu have made a difference in local attitudes. For example, community development initiatives, such as joint infrastructure construction and group credit schemes, have arisen independently of the research project. Communities now take more initiative and have a more active voice in local government decisions. This is a substantial change from previous practices of top-down communications.

While traditional on-station crop research at RNRRC continues, research managers have learned from experience, and now use a more participatory approach to ensure that their work is relevant to local farmers' needs. There are other changes as well. Social scientists are now part of the mix, strengthening the team's participatory research skills. And there is a firm commitment to a broad expansion of community-based natural resource management research to support rural livelihoods throughout Bhutan.

The experiences of Lingmutey Chu have been widely shared and have had a significant impact on the national research system and on national government policy. In a wide range of problem areas — from nontimber forest products to livestock management and irrigation — community-based participatory action research is being used to explore practical ways to implement a national policy commitment to decentralized, community-based NRM. As with water management, the national government recognizes that, to meet its NRM obligations, it sometimes must turn over more authority and responsibility to local communities.

CHINA: participatory rural poverty reduction in Guizhou

Researchers did away with the traditional top-down, highly bureaucratic approach to rural service delivery. Instead they tapped poor farmers' local knowledge and helped them introduce new crops, as well as institutional mechanisms for marketing produce and managing resources such as water.

Methodology: participatory planning, monitoring, and evaluation

Livelihoods: increased grain production, new high-value market crops, improved water supply

Governance: new resource-management institutions, new relations with local government

Partnerships and networks: village initiatives are attracting attention of other communities and serving as a platform for NGO investments

Policy: people-centred rural development

Battling the bureaucracy

Although tiny Bhutan is dwarfed by its giant northern neighbour, China, the problems faced by villagers on both sides of the border appear similar. Take Guizhou province in southwestern China (Figure 8). It is one of the poorest regions of the country. Its mountainous countryside is inhabited mostly by ethnic minority peoples. They manage complex production systems that include irrigated and rain-fed rice, forests, pastures, and unproductive wastelands.

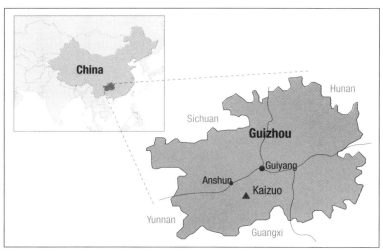

Figure 8. Guizhou, China.

But any similarity between Lingmutey Chu and Guizhou is only superficial. The problems of this region of China run much deeper. Hillsides were denuded by misguided industrial development plans in the central government's "Great Leap Forward" during the 1950s, and it has proven extremely difficult to re-establish forests, improve crop yields, and diversify production systems on the thin soils covering porous limestone rock.

Today, the rural economy of China has been largely transformed: cultivated lands were transferred to farmers under the "household responsibility" system, markets have been opened up, and farmers have a choice in what they can produce and how. Forests, grasslands, and sources of water in rural areas remain under government control. Local communities have constitutional rights to manage these common pool resources, but little attention has been paid to institutional arrangements that would support such collective management.

Government programs and services were developed and delivered in a top-down fashion that ignored local knowledge and customary practices. The result was predictable: "We have not held a community meeting in a long time," says an apathetic villager. "The government usually makes the decisions for us."

Some researchers at the Guizhou Academy of Agricultural Sciences (GAAS), however, were determined to try new, integrated research strategies. With support from IDRC, they selected a number of villages in Kaizuo Township — an impoverished area where local government had given up on prospects for improving livelihoods. Attempts to increase agricultural production, focusing on plant breeding and growth, had failed because they did not meet the needs of farmers.

The new GAAS team was made up of enthusiastic young researchers who were willing to learn, to try new methods, to spend long periods of time in difficult fieldwork with villagers, and who had a broad range of disciplinary skills. Their novel participatory approach built on local knowledge by strengthening the capacities of farmers and organizing communities to support new resource management institutions.

Self-confidence and independence

The researchers encouraged open village discussion of the problems and alternative management strategies. They engaged groups of resource users to work together with village leaders on implementing and enforcing management rules. They used participatory diagnostic tools to assess resource management problems, and worked with local farmers to test a variety of technology options.

New products were introduced, such as mushrooms and specialty fruits that could be cultivated and sold by local women in nearby markets. But for the women to get involved in marketing they needed help to strengthen their literacy and numeracy skills. Most had little experience outside their own villages, had seldom visited market towns, and were unfamiliar with trading. Working together to organize the marketing of their produce not only increased the women's self-confidence but also strengthened social organization and practical livelihood skills, and greatly increased their incomes and independence.

Another important step was the move to collective investment and management of local infrastructure. This supported improvements such as water supply, irrigation, and road construction that would normally be undertaken by local government. For example, when government engineers turned down a request to improve the water supply in one village, the villagers themselves explored nearby water sources. With the help of the research team, they developed their own water supply distribution system, contributing their own labour and materials for construction. Even more significant, they organized a system to recover costs through metering

> "Now that we have begun to organize to manage our resources, we are seeing more and more benefits."

household use. Revenues were applied to system maintenance, with public financial records to build transparency and trust.

In only a couple of years, these improvements paid off for the villagers. Incomes increased and there was visible improvement in resource quality. The project attracted the attention of neighbouring villages, which requested similar support. Chinese and international NGOs became interested in working in the area because of the strength of community organizations.

The research team encouraged the villagers to monitor the implementation of projects themselves, so as to make early modifications if required. One of the unexpected results was that the behaviour and expectations of villagers about local governance changed. They began to articulate their needs more clearly and were better able to take initiative and use evidence to support their arguments for more responsive local government. "Now that we have begun to organize to manage our resources, we are seeing more and more benefits" was typical of the comments overheard by the researchers.

The research team frequently invited government officials from various agencies to attend meetings and kept them informed of their local innovations. Government staff were supportive, but generally too busy to get much involved in these activities, which they saw as being outside their specific responsibilities. "I am interested in being involved, but there are so many important tasks I must finish," said one harried bureaucrat. "Otherwise I will have problems in passing the annual evaluation."

Disseminating the knowledge

In 2001, after several years of action research in six villages, the GAAS researchers had gained substantial knowledge of how to reduce poverty through community-based natural resource management (CBNRM). They determined to devote more attention to disseminating this knowledge through the large and complex system of government administration.

The researchers encountered some success at the local level, where township officials were increasingly interested in the new methods. Said one township leader: "After we adopted the CBNRM approach, many management activities were done by the villagers. The government has been released from some tasks. The villagers now take care of themselves."

Higher up the bureaucratic ladder, however, the researchers found it a challenge to convince government staff. Despite the successes of the experienced research team, consistency with national policy, and the commitments of senior government officials, county officials strongly preferred not to implement these new practices. Their conventional administration mitigated against meaningful local participation. Commented one official: "If we give all the decision-making power to the villagers, what are we going to do? We will lose our jobs!"

> "If we give all the decision-making power to the villagers, what are we going to do? We will lose our jobs!"

On the other hand, horizontal transfer of participatory local management lessons worked well. Farmer-to-farmer and village-to-village learning proved very effective in motivating local initiative and innovation. And as township officials gained experience with approaches that gave more authority and responsibility to local people, they became more enthusiastic. By 2004, despite the reluctance at the county level, 29 of 37 communes in Kaizuo Township had experience with collaborative local management ventures and 30 formal management agreements had been approved. Over 600 ha of forests had been successfully planted and were growing under local management. Rice and corn production had increased sharply with the introduction of various high-yielding hybrid varieties. Over 65 ha of new, high-value fruit crops were cultivated. Four villages had established their own livestock banks, avoiding high-cost credit. Nine new drinking water supply systems had benefited 550 poor households.

On the Web
THE RESEARCH

Comanagement of natural resources requires decentralization and changing senior government staff approaches. Participatory research strategies pointed to practical innovations for extension and comanagement of forests, water, and irrigation systems, and to local governance reforms. However, it has proven easier in China to introduce these mechanisms at the local level, where government staff are more accountable and closer to the people most affected.

LEBANON: resource conflicts and changing livelihoods in Arsaal

A mix of communication methods — traditional face-to-face negotiation, consensus building, video, art, and brochures — proved effective in getting pastoralists and orchard owners to resolve longstanding conflicts over land use.

Key features of the research

Methodology: multidisciplinary, participatory research, participatory GIS, use of video in conflict management

Livelihoods: livestock improvement, orchard management, leguminous forage intercropping, livelihood activities for women

Rights: documented the enclosure of common pool resources

Governance: new organizations and processes for conflict management, new relations between resource users and local government

Partnerships and networks: local users' network as a basis for community organization and a platform for investments by other donors and NGOs

Coping with chaos

The sprawling rural watershed of Arsaal in the northeast corner of Lebanon is remote, mountainous, and sparsely populated (Figure 9). Although it lies only a few hours' drive from Beirut, its people are isolated in both religious and political terms from the rest of the country. Unlike their Chinese counterparts in Guizhou who faced stifling government bureaucracy, the Arsaali people lived for decades with virtually no government.

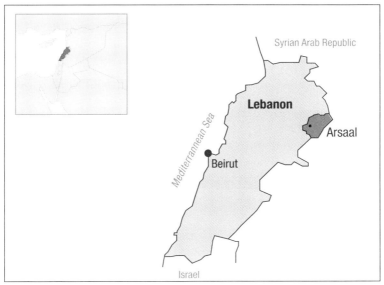

Figure 9. Arsaal, Lebanon.

For centuries, goats, sheep, and low-input cereal agriculture were
the main sources of income in the region. But since the 1960s,
some landowners have found it increasingly profitable to plant
rain-fed fruit orchards producing high-value stone fruit, such as
cherries and apricots, for urban markets. This conversion was
noted by researchers from the International Center for Agricultural Research in the Dry Areas (ICARDA) in an IDRC-funded
regional study of agricultural changes in the early 1990s. The
results also attracted the interest of an emerging multidisciplinary
environmental research group at the American University of
Beirut (AUB). With IDRC support, they set out to explore the
socioeconomic and biophysical sustainability of the changes in
Arsaal.

The researchers found numerous sources of conflict in the region,
many of them rooted in changes that had taken place over many
decades. The pastoral system had relied on traditional clan-based
relationships between large- and small-scale herders, and on

consensus decisions about the use of common pastures. That complex system had provided for flexible use of cultivated land, grazing lands, and tree fodder on lands at differing altitudes depending on season and rainfall.

However, these practices gradually broke down under increased grazing pressure and creeping enclosure. Orchards offered higher returns with much less labour. But, as a result, shortages of fodder became especially critical in dry years. Orchards also contributed to land degradation because of cultivation on fragile sloping pastureland. In the mid-1960s, the conflicts created by the changes contributed to the dissolution of the municipal council. With growing political and military conflict throughout Lebanon in the next decades, formal local elections were not held for 33 years, and the functions of local government largely dissolved.

Taking advantage of the power vacuum, some local and external entrepreneurs appropriated government land to open limestone quarries as a source of stone to face new buildings in Lebanon's reviving cities. Some quarries overlapped with the most productive ecological zone in the watershed. The quarry operations and the heavy trucks that hauled equipment and stone were a major source of dust, which coated leaves and fruit, reducing pasture and orchard productivity.

These rapid changes in the social and livelihood systems, combined with traditional clan animosities and differences of class, generation, ethnicity, and religion, served to entrench conflicts and impoverish those with the least power. "The disruption of the original pastoral system was nothing short of chaotic," according to Shadi Hamadeh, principal investigator for the AUB research team. "In many instances these events coincided with periods during which there was a lack of local authority. Simply put, nobody was there to regulate all of this."

> In many instances ... there was a total lack of authority. Simply put, nobody was there to regulate all of this."

Inspired by tradition

In the absence of effective government structures in Arsaal that might support better resource management, the researchers sought ways to make agriculture more sustainable and reduce land use conflicts. For inspiration, they turned to traditional tribal pasture-management practices. These involved consultation, face-to-face negotiations, and consensus building within the traditional *majlis,* or community councils.

The researchers worked with local community leaders and with the Arsaal Rural Development Association (ARDA), a local NGO, to help them establish a Local Users Network (LUN) inspired by the *majlis.* The network was a flexible structure that brought together various groups for face-to-face discussions of resource management problems. Among the direct stakeholders were pastoralists, orchard owners, men and women from the community, traditional decision-makers, and new local power figures. Outside researchers and development project staff also participated.

Learning tools included discussions, interviews, and on-farm trials led by researchers and farmers. The researchers emphasized communications among resource users themselves and between users and researchers. Communications media included video and art, as well as brochures, and engaged youth in the community to build environmental awareness. In each area of activity, researchers helped farmers and local leaders to design and test resource management interventions to secure livelihoods and reduce degradation. The results were highly relevant and widely disseminated to local users.

Video solutions

A key success of the LUN was its ability to help pastoralists and orchard growers reach solutions to their decades-old conflicts. The researchers used video interviews with the stakeholders to expose issues and challenge assumptions in ways that would not have been possible in face-to-face discussions, and would have been culturally inappropriate in the formal setting of a public meeting. "Through the process of making the video, people became much more candid," says Hamadeh. "By getting people to voice their real opinions about the conflict we became sure the problem wasn't confined to clans."

Now that they were sure of where the real issues lay, the researchers provided a common GIS database for all sides to use in their discussions. The also helped by suggesting win–win solutions — such as intercropping leguminous forages in the orchards to provide fodder and improve the soil at the same time. As local people gained confidence and experience in the process, they hosted groups of visiting farmers and officials from other parts of the Arab region. The LUN has since served as a model for the establishment of similar community-based organizations in several other parts of the region.

> The Local Users Network has served as a model for the establishment of similar community-based organizations in several other regions.

Institutional innovations

A key outcome when local government was reconstituted in 1999 was that many of the newly elected councilors came from the ranks of LUN leaders. However, the main focus of the LUN remains research and shared learning, not political involvement. The research team continued to develop new GIS tools to assess and prioritize land degradation issues using local knowledge. They worked with orchard growers to build understanding of the nature and causes of land degradation and to help identify areas of potential expansion with the least risk of degradation.

While the project researchers worked hard to introduce improved management technologies to benefit local farmers, the most significant innovations in Arsaal were undoubtedly institutional. The LUN, for example, created a forum for discussing problems and introducing new ideas to strengthen livelihoods, such as a herders' cooperative (the first in Lebanon) and a women's cooperative. The latter focused on processing fruits and weaving carpets to add value to local agricultural products.

The project also served as a model for new research methods and processes and led to AUB creating a new Environment and Sustainable Development Unit. This unit undertakes multi-disciplinary, participatory research on dryland areas, hosts several large community development projects, and provides regional leadership in networking on participatory and community development.

At the national level, Arsaal continues to be regarded as a remote and marginal area of little interest to highly politicized government agencies. But the new local government, together with resource user groups, has been able to influence policies. For example, they were able to thwart proposed central government support for further development of the quarrying industry in the region. Together, the local council and the new resource user groups and networks have established the institutional foundations for shared learning and resource sustainability using the tools generated by the research project.

On the Web
THE RESEARCH

Part 4

Outcomes, Lessons, and Challenges

These six cases are but a small sample from a substantial portfolio of IDRC-supported research projects that have addressed the confluence of rural poverty and environmental degradation. While resource management has been the subject of much theoretical and analytical research by many organizations, the IDRC cases are striking because of their emphasis on practice. Their measure of success has not been what the scientists learned. Rather, it has been the lessons adapted and implemented by local women and men. Despite their differences in culture, politics, and ecology, the cases have common outcomes and they provide recurring lessons for development practitioners whose job it is to tackle poverty and environmental issues.

Research outcomes

The project teams recognized there are no off-the-shelf solutions to the complex problems of resource management and productivity in marginal areas. They had to suspend their assumptions and embrace the unique situation of their local partners as their starting point. Among the key questions the scientists had to answer at the outset were: Who is using which resources? What kinds of access rights do they have?

The researchers needed to build the trust and engagement of local people by helping them secure their livelihoods and increase the productivity of their resources. But beyond that, they had to demonstrate to their local partners that there would be long-term access to the resources and that the benefits of improved resource management would not be ephemeral.

To sustain the benefits and quality of the resource base, new institutions for local resource management and governance were required. In many cases, local lessons pointed to the need for policy reforms in resource tenure or governance. In all of these innovations, the knowledge, learning, and leadership of local women and men were pivotal.

All the research projects addressed longer term livelihood security for the rural poor by delivering three kinds of outcomes:

➤ More secure access to the resources on which the poor typically depend;

➤ New institutions for resource governance that give poor local users a greater voice; and

➤ New technologies to boost resource productivity.

In China's Guizhou province, for example, research helped solve perennial, time-consuming problems of both domestic and irrigation water supply. This led to direct improvements in local livelihoods. The crucial innovation was a new local institutional mechanism for farmers to finance and install a water-distribution system. With a regular supply of water secured, they were then able to start cultivating fruit on previously unproductive land.

Farmer Lu Quan from the village of Dongkou summed up the gains: "Because of the management of the (new) tap water system, women have to work less. Overall, we have saved 540 hours of labour in the dry season, per year. ... We have invested our labour and money in the orchards. Now we are learning more about cultivation and management and marketing skills. We want to produce more fruit and make more money."

In Ecuador's El Angel watershed, research demonstrated the inadequacy of existing institutional mechanisms for planning and allocating water supply. But it also highlighted the value of having all water users protect their shared water source and improve the quality of water throughout the watershed. The project thereby stimulated interest in a new multistakeholder management platform. This innovation in local governance based its success on improved technologies for water monitoring and use in order to ensure equitable access to the resource.

Research outcomes in the three categories — secure access, new institutions, and technology for higher productivity — are thus tightly interconnected. The Vietnamese case illustrates these linkages. Mobile gear fishers in the Tam Giang Lagoon learned how to raise valuable grass carp in pens. But for this new technology to be productive, the aquaculturists and the fish corral owners had to agree on lagoon use and monitoring. Production zones for fish pens, habitat protection areas for sea grass (essential to wild fish fry and as a feed source), and waterway navigation channels all had to be allocated among various users. And the arrangements had to take account of lagoon nutrient flows and currents. All this would have been impossible without the new data provided by researchers and the institutional innovations linked to comanagement. The latter included participatory planning, data sharing, technical support, and sanctions from government. The effectiveness of these research outcomes, in Viet Nam and elsewhere, was not due to any single component, but rather to the interaction of complementary innovations.

The same kinds of linked outcomes are also evident in the other cases. A summary is presented on page 71. It shows how participatory action research by each site-based team led to significant changes in the institutional framework and practice of resource management. The striking element in all the cases is that the resulting actions or interventions were not undertaken by the researchers but by local resource users and governments. Through meaningful engagement in action learning, local farmers, fishers, and government staff were able to change their perceptions to introduce innovations not previously possible.

Many innovations centred on better governance — ways to manage conflicts over resources, make decisions more transparent and decision-makers more accountable, increase the representation of marginalized social groups, and create higher expectations for the behaviour of local officials. These institutional changes are highly relevant as central governments everywhere come under pressure to decentralize and democratize decision-making. Such changes are notoriously difficult to implement when public officials have no alternative models and are accustomed to exercising tight control. The IDRC cases show how constructive new roles can be built for government in facilitating, advising, and providing technical support and sanctions for resource comanagement.

> The effectiveness of these outcomes was not due to any single component, but rather to the interaction of complementary innovations.

As beneficial as the results on the ground have been, the projects also expanded the capacity, the skills, and even the roles of the researchers themselves. The researchers had to develop new methods and work across disciplinary divides. They learned how to learn from local people. They gained practical skills in conflict

Summary of selected research outcomes to increase livelihood security through resource management

Research outcome	Cambodia	Viet Nam	Bhutan	China	Lebanon	Ecuador
Secure access to resources	Customary land tenure enshrined in new legislation Community forest recognized	Rights of mobile-gear fishers recognized Pen and net enclosures legitimized	Downstream users secured access to water	Local initiatives for collective development of water, forests, roads	Tenure conflicts reduced Grazing access strengthened	Water sources, water allocation, and land tenure security improved
Institutions for resource governance	Participatory land use planning Local resource management committees	Fishing coalition and user groups Multistakeholder planning process	Watershed consultative group Community forestry committees	Village-based management units for infrastructure Collective action for water and land management	Consultative multi-stakeholder group Cooperatives	Consultative multistakeholder roundtable Water allocation negotiations
Benefits delivered to community	Community plans enable better access to government and donor investment funds	Introduced fish pens Reduced destructive fishing practices Improved agriculture	Irrigation canals improved Community forest plantations Rice production	Water supply Grain production Fruit production Fodder	Livestock herds improved Fodder production increased Processing introduced	Water supply system improved Agricultural systems strengthened
Linkages	Research demonstrated customary management and built support for policy change Secure tenure and new institutions provide a platform for agricultural extension and local government reforms	Research created awareness of linked problems in lagoon Improved production systems required collective planning process linking users with local and provincial governments	Research showed water availability and inequitable allocation Policy changes, new institutions for negotiating water supply, and reliable water meant increased rice production	Productivity improvements led to gains in income and confidence Collective action strengthened access to water, forests, and markets to consolidate income gains	Consultative forum allowed sharing of research results to reduce conflicts Technical inputs improved productivity Collective action needed for pasture improvement All built capacity for local governance	Research results increased transparency in water system Information shared via roundtable Collective action and negotiation facilitated
Other major outcomes	Networks for sharing research results Innovations and policy advocacy	Model for implementing comanagement policy	Major changes to research methods Contribution to national CBNRM policy	Introduced participatory rural development tools and farmer-to-farmer learning to local government	New research methods and tools New interdisciplinary research unit at American University of Beirut	Strengthening local government Building interdisciplinary research capacity

On the Web
THE LESSONS

management and learned to communicate cross-culturally. They developed tools for integrating research results so that complex biophysical and spatial analyses could respond to the practical demands of local resource users and other actors. They had to subject their work to the critical review not just of their academic peers, but of hard-nosed farmers whose precarious livelihoods leave little room for misjudgement. And they adopted new roles as facilitators of local learning and adaptation.

An important accomplishment of these research projects has been the development of new field methods and capacities for participatory, integrated, and interdisciplinary research within organizations where these did not previously exist. In all cases, the experience transformed the research teams and their organizations. It resulted in new standards and sometimes led to the establishment of specialized new research groups that are now engaged in other projects.

Dr Nuhad Daghir, Dean of the Faculty of Agriculture and Food Sciences at the American University of Beirut, reflects on the impact of the Arsaal research project on learning and development practice: "This experience, which was developed in farmers' fields, is now being integrated into our academic programs. ... More emphasis is being placed on environmental preservation and protection, and on the social and cultural aspects of farming life. The newly created Environment and Sustainable Development Unit is deeply involved in development projects targeting the poor and supporting rural livelihoods. These projects have become the national and regional reference in the enhancement of the livelihoods of small farmers."

Beyond creating new knowledge, technologies, and practices, the IDRC-supported research projects stimulated new ways of thinking about the very kinds of knowledge needed to manage natural resources wisely. They transformed the systems and institutions by which people and organizations made decisions. They introduced the foundations for comanagement.

Lessons

These research experiences show that even in very difficult contexts it is possible to introduce successful natural resource comanagement schemes. Substantial investments in time-consuming learning-by-doing and capacity building paid off — but not just for the communities. The research teams have learned to be more effective and some of them are already making good use of their experience, applying it at other sites more quickly and easily. What are their lessons for comanagement?

1. Put people at the centre.

Practitioners and researchers concerned about poverty and resource management should put poor people at the centre of their work. Lasting solutions must be driven by the knowledge, experience, and action of local people. To achieve change which could never be imposed from outside requires meaningful engagement of local resource users and other stakeholders — men and women, poor and wealthy, community leaders and government officials, farmers and fishers — in knowledge generation with researchers. But this kind of participatory action research demands more of both researchers and practitioners. Development agencies and research organizations need a better approach to learning.

2. Learn by doing.

New resource management strategies should build on knowledge gained through practice and application by users, as well as knowledge acquired by researchers. New tools and methods are essential to this effort, as are attitudes of recognition and mutual respect. Experimentation remains essential to the research effort, and scientific methods remain crucial in evaluating experimental outcomes. Farmers and fishers, as well as development practitioners and their organizations, would benefit from mechanisms to reduce the risks of experimentation and formalize shared learning.

3. Secure access to resources for local communities.

With a people-centred approach to shared learning by doing, **comanagement interventions need to start by recognizing rights and securing access to resources.** Rights can be built on traditional values and social obligations, but they also need to have legal standing and state support. The challenge here is to develop secure collective tenure for the common pool resources that are essential to ecosystem productivity and livelihoods but difficult to manage. Because any system of collective resource tenure must provide for enforcement and conflict management, it must be premised on local legitimacy and social practices as well as legality.

4. Build new institutions for resource management.

Effective management of common pool resources requires institutions for collective action. It is an exercise quite different from the management of private tenure: it demands new processes of local governance. Close attention must be paid to issues of representation, equity, accountability, and transparency. Local organizations can contribute to these innovations, which rarely take shape by themselves. Education, organizational support, leadership development, and technical advice may all be needed to build community organizations and governance processes for comanagement. Participatory action research is a powerful tool in this task.

5. Find innovations that deliver early returns.

Community and organizational development are long-term processes requiring the confidence and trust of local groups. One way to show the value of such efforts and the potential gains from resource comanagement is to **respond to the urgent livelihood needs of the poor by delivering benefits.** These may derive from improved production technologies or high-value products, or even from compensation for ecosystem services. Some of these may require collective effort. Others may be managed by individual households using private or common pool resources. In the cases cited, the responsiveness of the research teams was an important factor in local success.

6. Build linkages and networks.

While direct building of organizational capacity is essential, community groups need much more support than that. For action research and adaptive learning, for political support and advocacy, for public awareness and education, **local organizations need to be able to tap into broader networks and create new partnerships.** In all the cases cited, these resources extended well beyond the local IDRC project research teams. They included NGOs, government agencies, like-minded local governments in other areas, and even international networks and donors. Such networks are valuable sources of technical information and models for reform, and they serve as venues for organizing exchange visits and sometimes exerting political pressure. These factors all contribute to the success of local institutional innovations.

On the Web
THE LESSONS

7. Innovations must be interdisciplinary.

The complex problems of poverty and environmental degradation can be successfully tackled by innovation. In all the cases, the insights of scientists were instrumental in creating new options for livelihood security. By themselves, though, technical insights are not enough. Every case demonstrates that livelihood security also requires transforming inequitable institutional structures and processes. **If research is to respond to the practical and political constraints faced by the poor, social and institutional analysis must mesh with biophysical and ecological studies.** New interdisciplinary approaches to research are essential to deliver multidimensional innovations. These need support from research organizations and donors.

8. Policies should enable local innovation.

A final lesson from community-based innovation: whereas practical improvements to livelihood security are essential to demonstrate success, **long-term resolution of local problems sometimes requires higher level policy reforms.** Interventions are needed at multiple scales: implementing change implies local action, but enabling conditions and coordination are often needed beyond that level to facilitate local change. The cases suggest that insufficient policy attention has been paid to securing collective resource rights as a means to ensure resource access and management for the poor.

Many governments are looking for ways to decentralize NRM effectively. The case studies show how innovative local institutions, with external and senior government support, can build the necessary foundations for this. The types of support needed to sustain comanagement innovations are enabling policies, technical advice and extension, monitoring, and enforcement. **Government failure to provide an enabling environment severely weakens local comanagement initiatives over the long term.**

Challenges

The case studies demonstrate that development organizations and research institutes are able to generate local comanagement innovations. Enabling policies to support community resource rights, along with broader application of participatory action research approaches, would be helpful. Focusing on local benefits while building broader networks is important. These approaches can be applied more widely by practitioners and community organizations. But the cases also reveal some of the people-related challenges in taking this approach.

Participatory methods require skilled management, keen observation, tact, and patience. It is always easier to engage powerful, outspoken resource users than to work with the poorest and most isolated, who also tend to be the most reserved. These participants-on-the-sidelines, often women and members of minority ethnic groups, may be so busy with family survival that they have little time for interacting with external facilitators.

Communication skills and language may pose barriers on both sides. Researchers and members of the community, even the marginalized themselves, may discount the value of their inputs. Social conventions may render these people almost invisible in a community: uncounted, unmentionable, unconsulted. This can be a very difficult situation for researchers to overcome. Social relations, historical prejudices, and relationships of exchange and political loyalty cannot be dismissed. They are essential elements of any community's social structure. Participatory researchers must be careful not to entrench existing power structures or to exacerbate inequities through their work.

On the Web
THE LESSONS

Although researchers on the projects made considerable efforts to identify and address women's issues in natural resource management, they were only partially successful. Deep-seated social structures and inequities do not change overnight. And without a particular focus on the problems of marginalized people, it is easy for their concerns to become camouflaged in the larger thicket of NRM issues.

> It is always easier to engage powerful, outspoken resource users than to work with the poorest and most isolated. … Social conventions may render these people almost invisible in a community: uncounted, unmentionable, unconsulted.

The case studies do reveal examples of how women have benefited from the research interventions — through specific identification of women's issues, through targeted livelihood interventions, through greater transparency and access to decision-making, and through more responsive local governance. But most of the research groups acknowledged that the fundamental institutions of power and decision-making remain male-dominated and that gender-focused initiatives are still easily sidelined.

Participation is inherently political. It empowers people, but then is seen as a threat to the existing structure of authority, which will resist change. More broadly, rural development and poverty reduction are likewise processes of social change — part productivity improvement, part shift in power relations. Most governments recognize the value of these processes and officially encourage reforms. But when it comes to local interventions, researchers are well advised to be cautious about the motives of external actors, including their own.

One of the most challenging tasks in introducing comanagement institutions is to encourage change in government agencies, especially at the national level. The case study from China's Guizhou province reveals some of these issues. Large bureaucracies have an internal logic that resists innovation and frequently rewards the concentration of power more than effective programming. Some of the cases illustrate how evidence-based policy arguments (as in Cambodia and Bhutan) can turn things around; but these succeeded because of effective external advocacy and the receptivity of government officials.

The six cases show that researchers have had a number of successes in both strengthening rural livelihoods and promoting the necessary institutional arrangements for comanagement of natural resources. Are these successes sustainable? What other significant effects, positive or negative, might emerge?

Longer term monitoring of ecological, social, and political change can help answer these questions. Going a step further, any comanagement structure will also have to be able to adapt to changing ecological, market, social, and policy conditions. In many of the research sites, these monitoring, evaluation, and adaptation mechanisms and cycles are taking shape, having been built into the comanagement strategy from the outset. They will tell the tale in the final analysis. Patience is required, not just because some ecosystems are slow to respond to stimuli, but also because human knowledge of the things "managed" and of the "managers" themselves is so limited. In the face of continued change, local resource users will be able to adopt more sustainable and productive practices only if they continue to learn and change. The practice of participatory action research builds this adaptive learning capacity.

Glossary of Terms and Acronyms

Action learning: A research strategy that formalizes processes for mutual learning and local innovation by multiple, complementary actors on the basis of shared knowledge and action.

Adaptive comanagement: A system of management in which multiple parties are involved in different ways in a process of iterative problem solving. Learning from shared experience and analysis informs subsequent action, information gathering, and management decisions.

ARDA: Arsaal Rural Development Association, Lebanon

AUB: American University of Beirut, Lebanon (www.aub.edu.lb)

CBNRM: Community-based natural resource management

CIDA: Canadian International Development Agency (www.acdi-cida.gc.ca)

Comanagement: A collaborative arrangement in which the community of local resource users, local and senior governments, other stakeholders, and external actors share responsibility and authority for management of the natural resource in question. Comanagement covers a spectrum of arrangements — from politically negotiated formal legal agreements to informal pragmatic deals.

Common pool resources: Resources whose ecological characteristics make them very difficult for any individual to manage (for example, as a result of mobility, scale, overlap of multiple resources and users, or difficulty of exclusion).

Common property: A system of collective rights to resources that permits the management of a clearly identified common pool resource by a defined social group.

CPRs: common pool resources

Customary (or traditional) rights: Locally recognized by a defined social group, but not necessarily codified in written or legal form. They are typically related to long-standing cultural practices and social relations (clan or family, patron–client, or other hierarchies). They may change over time, but can still be effectively enforced.

GAAS: Guizhou Academy of Agricultural Sciences, China

GIS: geographic information system

HUAF: Hue University of Agriculture and Forestry, Viet Nam (www.hueuni.edu.vn/en/agriculture.htm)

ICARDA: International Center for Agricultural Research in the Dry Areas, Syria (www.icarda.org)

IDRC: International Development Research Centre, Canada (www.idrc.ca)

IIRR: International Institute of Rural Reconstruction, Philippines (www.iirr.org)

Local government: The lowest level of formal state institutions, such as district-level officials or local, publicly accountable decision-making and service-delivery organizations constituted in accordance with national laws (such as in local elections). Local government structures take different forms in different countries and vary in their levels of accountability to local people or to senior governments.

LUN: Local Users Network, Arsaal, Lebanon

NGO: nongovernmental organization

NRM: natural resource management

Open access: A system of resource tenure for common pool resources in which other users cannot be excluded, effectively precluding management or conservation.

Participatory research: Doing research with people, rather than for people. This approach treats natural resource users (men and women, farmers, fishers, forest users) as collaborative learners. There is a wide range of learning methods that may be used (including appraisal, mapping, monitoring, and evaluation), but they are all characterized by a fundamentally different relationship between the researcher and the people involved than is the case in traditional, expert-driven research. This difference often requires changes to the roles, processes, and structure of scientific research organizations to enable effective implementation of participatory research methods (see Gonsalves et al. 2005).

RNRRC: Renewable Natural Resources Research Centre, Bhutan

SDC: Swiss Agency for Development and Cooperation (www.sdc.admin.ch)

UNDP: United Nations Development Programme (www.undp.org)

Sources and Resources

Cited References

Beck, T.; Nesmith, C. 2001. Building on poor people's capacities: the case of common property resources in India and West Africa. World Development, 29(1), 119–133.

Berkes, F., ed. 1989. Common property resources: ecology and community-based sustainable development. Bellhaven Press, London, UK.

Chambers, R. 1997. Whose reality counts: putting the first last. Bath Press, Bath, UK.

Flaherty, M.; Vandergeest, P.; Miller, P. 1999. Rice paddy or shrimp pond: tough decisions in rural Thailand. World Development, 27(12), 2045–2060.

Goetze, T.C. 2004. Sharing the Canadian experience with comanagement: ideas, examples and lessons for communities in developing areas. International Development Research Centre, Ottawa, Canada. RPE Working Paper Series. Online: www.idrc.ca/en/ev-82096-201-1-DO_TOPIC.html

Gonsalves, J.; Becker, T; Braun, A; Campilan, D.; De Chavez, H.; Fajber, E.; Kapiriri, M.; Rivaca-Caminade, J.; Vernooy, R., ed. 2005. Participatory research and development for sustainable agriculture and natural resource management. International Potato Center — Users/ Perspectives with Agricultural Research and Development, Laguna, Philippines, and International Development Research Centre, Ottawa, Canada. Online: www.idrc.ca/en/ev-84706-201-1-DO_TOPIC.html

O'Hara, P. 2006. Shaping the key to fit the lock: participatory action research and community forestry in the Philippines. *In* Tyler, S.R., ed., Communities, livelihoods, and natural resources: action research and policy change in Asia. ITDG Publishing, London, UK, and International Development Research Centre, Ottawa, Canada. Online: www.idrc.ca/en/ev-97782-201-1-DO_TOPIC.html

Ostrom, E. 1990. Governing the commons: the evolution of institutions for collective action. Cambridge University Press, Cambridge, UK.

Leach, M.; Mearns, R.; Scoones, I. 1999. Environmental entitlements: dynamics and institutions in community-based natural resource management. World Development, 27(2), 225–247.

Schlager, E.; Ostrom, E. 1992. Property-rights regimes and natural resources: a conceptual analysis. Land Economics, 68(3), 249–262.

Vandergeest, P. 1997. Rethinking property. Common Property Resource Digest, 41, 4–6.

Varughese, G. 2000. Population and forest dynamics in the hills of Nepal: institutional remedies by rural communities. *In* Gibson, C.C.; McKean, M.A.; Ostrom, E., ed., People and forests: communities, institutions, and governance. MIT Press, Cambridge, MA, USA. pp. 193–226.

Vernooy, R., ed. 2006. Social and gender analysis in natural resource management: learning studies and lessons from Asia. Sage India, New Delhi, India, and International Development Research Centre, Ottawa, Canada. Online: www.idrc.ca/en/ev-91907-201-1-DO_TOPIC.html

WCED (World Commission on Environment and Development). 1987. Our common future. Oxford University Press, Oxford, UK.

Related Reading

Berkes, F.; George, P.; Preston, R. 1991. Comanagement: the evolution in theory and practice of the joint administration of living resources. Alternatives, 18(2), 12–18.

Borrini-Feyerabend, G.; Pimbert, M.; Farvar, M.T.; Kothari, A.; Renard, Y. 2004. Sharing power: learning-by-doing in comanagement of natural resources throughout the world. IIED and IUCN/CEESP/CMWG, Cenesta, Tehran.

Buckles, D., ed. 1999. Cultivating peace: conflict and collaboration in natural resource management. International Development Research Centre, Ottawa, Canada. Online: www.idrc.ca/en/ev-9398-201-1-DO_TOPIC.html

Carlsson, L.; Berkes, F. 2005. Comanagement: concepts and methodological implications. Journal of Environmental Management, 75, 65–76.

Chambers, R.; Pacey, A.; Thrupp, L.A., ed. 1989. Farmer first: farmer innovation and agricultural research. ITDG Publishing, London, UK.

Grenier, L. 1998. Working with indigenous knowledge: a guide for researchers. International Development Research Centre, Ottawa, Canada. Online: www.idrc.ca/en/ev-9310-201-1-DO_TOPIC.html

Hamadeh, S.; Haider, M.; Zurayk, R. 2006. Research for development in the dry Arab regions: the cactus flower. International Development Research Centre, Ottawa, Canada. Online: www.idrc.ca/en/ev-93511-201-1-DO_TOPIC.html

Ken, S.R.; Carson, T.; Riebe, K.; Cox, S.; von Kaschke, E. 2005. CBNRM in Cambodia: selected papers on concepts and experiences. CBNRM Learning Institute, Phnom Penh, Cambodia.

Pinkerton, E.; Weinstein, M. 1995. Fisheries that work: sustainability through community-based management. David Suzuki Foundation, Vancouver, Canada.

Pomeroy, R. S.; Rivera-Guieb, R. 2006. Fishery comanagement: a practical handbook. CABI Publishers, Wallingford, UK, and International Development Research Centre, Ottawa, Canada. Online: www.idrc.ca/en/ev-92339-201-1-DO_TOPIC.html

Pound, B.; Snapp, S.; McDougall, C.; Braun, A., ed. 2003. Managing natural resources for sustainable development: uniting science and participation. Earthscan Publications Ltd., London, UK, and International Development Research Centre, Ottawa, Canada. Online: www.idrc.ca/en/ev-34000-201-1-DO_TOPIC.html

Sayer, J.; Campbell, B. 2004. The science of sustainable development: local livelihoods and the global environment. Cambridge University Press, Cambridge, UK.

Tyler, S.R., ed. 2006. Communities, livelihoods, and natural resources: action research and policy change in Asia. ITDG Publishing, London, UK, and International Development Research Centre, Ottawa, Canada. Online: www.idrc.ca/en/ev-97782-201-1-DO_TOPIC.html

Vernooy, R.; Sun Qiu; Xu Jianchu, ed. 2003. Voices for change: participatory monitoring and evaluation in China. Yunnan Science and Technology Press, Kunming, China, and International Development Research Centre, Ottawa, Canada. Online: www.idrc.ca/en/ev-26686-201-1-DO_TOPIC.html

Relevant Web sites

Environment and Sustainable Development Unit
Faculty of Agriculture and Food Sciences
American University of Beirut
Beirut, Lebanon
www.aub.edu.lb/~webeco/ESDU

EPINARM project
Renewable Natural Resources Research Centre, Bajo
Ministry of Agriculture
Royal Government of Bhutan
www.ires.ubc.ca/projects/lingmutey/html/main.htm

Manrecur Project
Grupo Randi-Randi
Quito, Ecuador
www.randirandi.org

Ministry of Agriculture
Royal Government of Bhutan
www.moa.gov.bt

Rural Poverty and the Environment Program Initiative
International Development Research Centre
Ottawa, Canada
www.idrc.ca/rpe

The Publisher

The International Development Research Centre is a public corporation created by the Parliament of Canada in 1970 to help researchers and communities in the developing world find solutions to their social, economic, and environmental problems. Support is directed toward developing an indigenous research capacity to sustain policies and technologies developing countries need to build healthier, more equitable, and more prosperous societies.

IDRC Books publishes research results and scholarly studies on global and regional issues related to sustainable and equitable development. As a specialist in development literature, IDRC Books contributes to the body of knowledge on these issues to further the cause of global understanding and equity. The full catalogue is available at www.idrc.ca/books.